KERBER

YANN TIERSEN

Artwork by Katy Ann Gilmore

ISBN: 978-1-70514-310-0

Visit Hal Leonard Online at
www.halleonard.com

Contact us:
Hal Leonard
7777 West Bluemound Road
Milwaukee, WI 53213
Email: info@halleonard.com

In Europe, contact:
Hal Leonard Europe Limited
42 Wigmore Street
Marylebone, London, W1U 2RY
Email: info@halleonardeurope.com

In Australia, contact:
Hal Leonard Australia Pty. Ltd.
4 Lentara Court
Cheltenham, Victoria, 3192 Australia
Email: info@halleonard.com.au

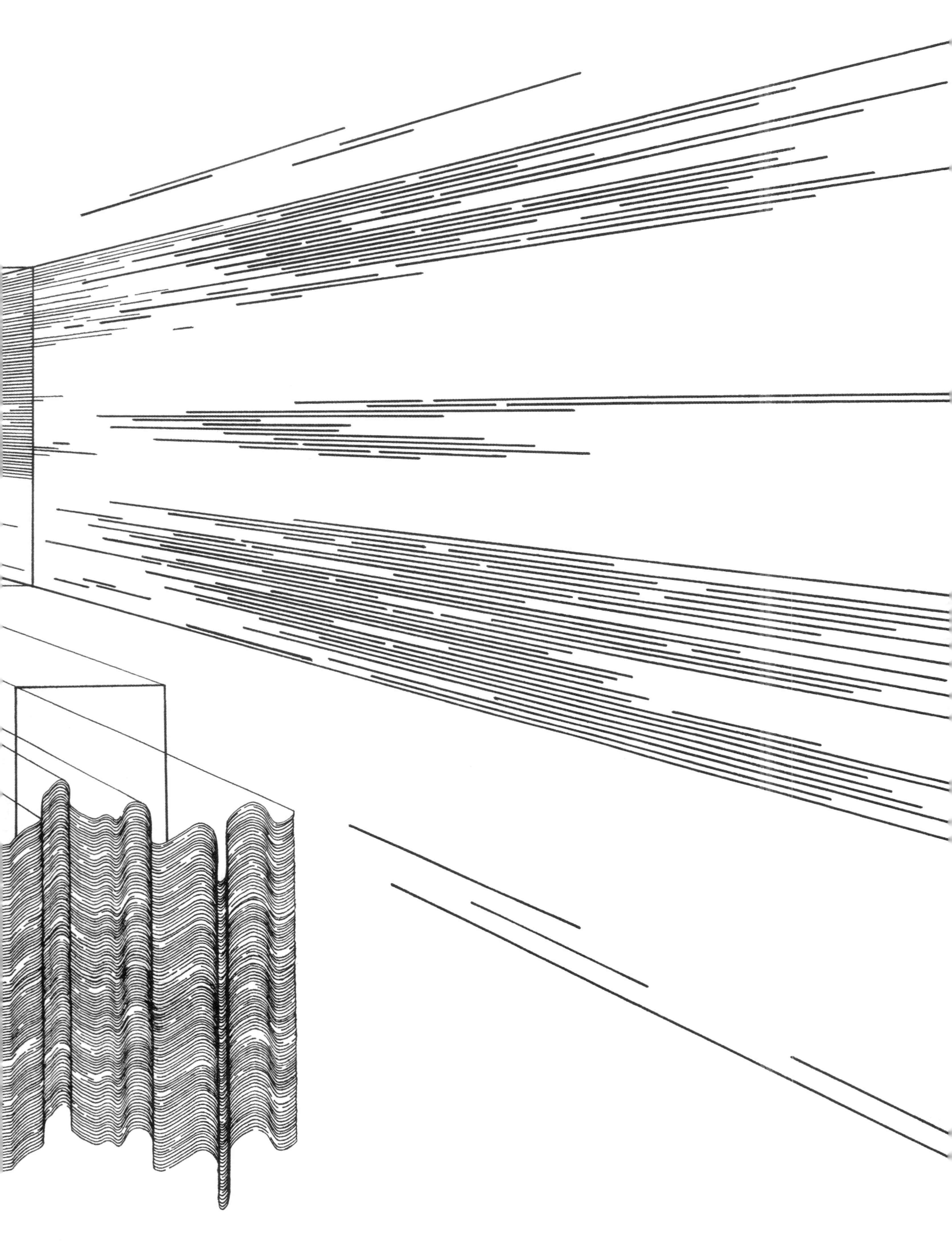

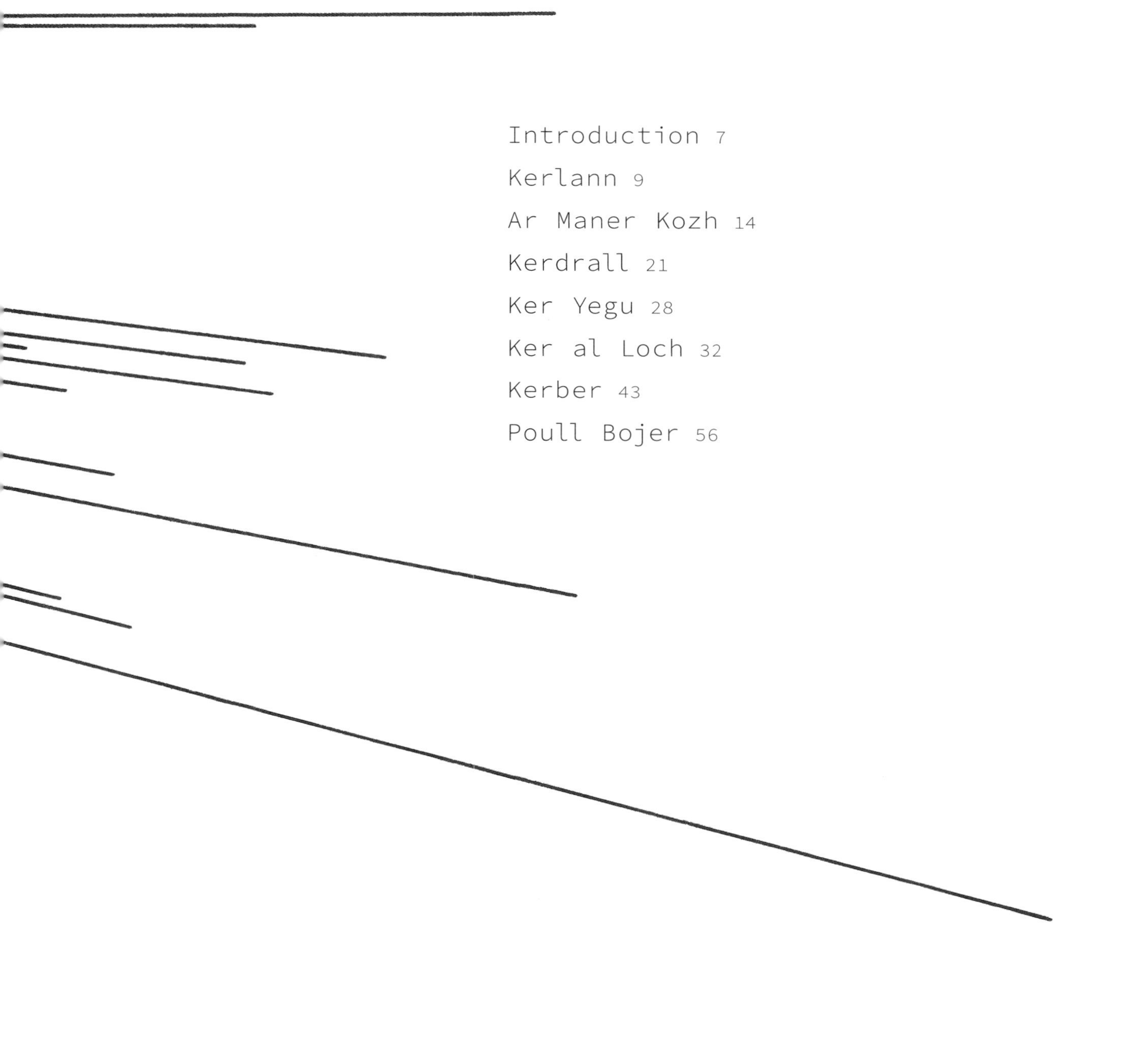

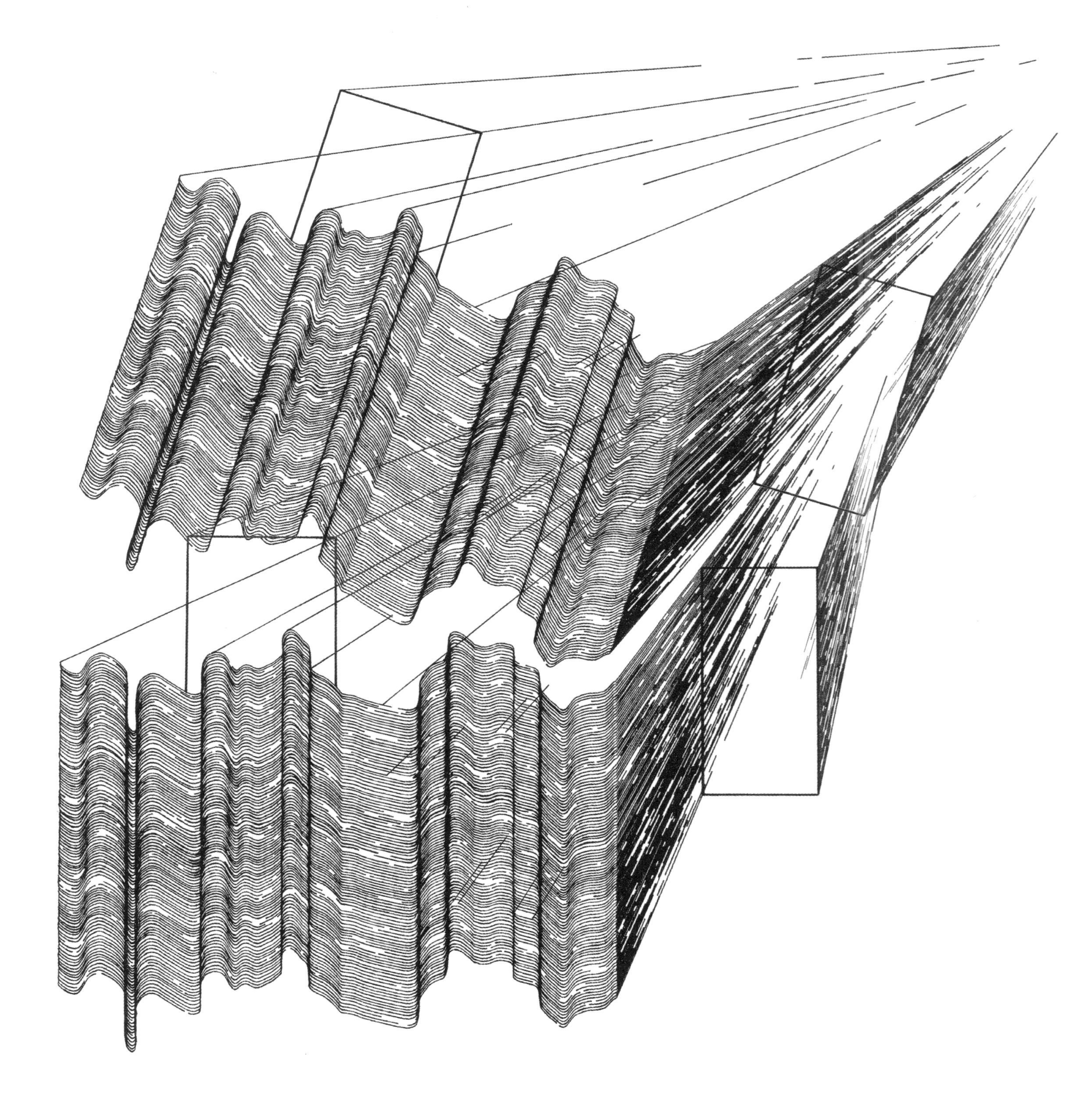

"I think there is a similarity between the infinite big and the infinite smallness of everything," explains Yann Tiersen, *"It's the same experiment looking through a microscope as it is a telescope."* This exploration of the micro and the macro has permeated through much of Tiersen's career, and his new collection of work, *Kerber*, once again shows the vast expansiveness and intricate detail of his work.

This new collection is closely connected to Ushant, the Breton island located 30 kilometres off the West coast of Brittany in the Celtic Sea that Tiersen calls home. *Kerber* is named after a chapel in a small village on the island and being further influenced by the close geographical area around him, each track is tied to a place mapping out the immediate landscape that surrounds Tiersen's home.

This isn't a collection about isolation, however, it's more an expression of being conscious of your own direct environment and your place within it—a sonic encapsulation of the hyper-local. For Tiersen, this approach extracts the same degree of profundity as spending the evening studying the stars—which he himself does. *"You can look at things that are thousands of light years away and relate your own existence to this really cosmic element,"* he says. *"But you get that same feeling with the things all around you."*

Kerlann

MUSIC BY YANN TIERSEN

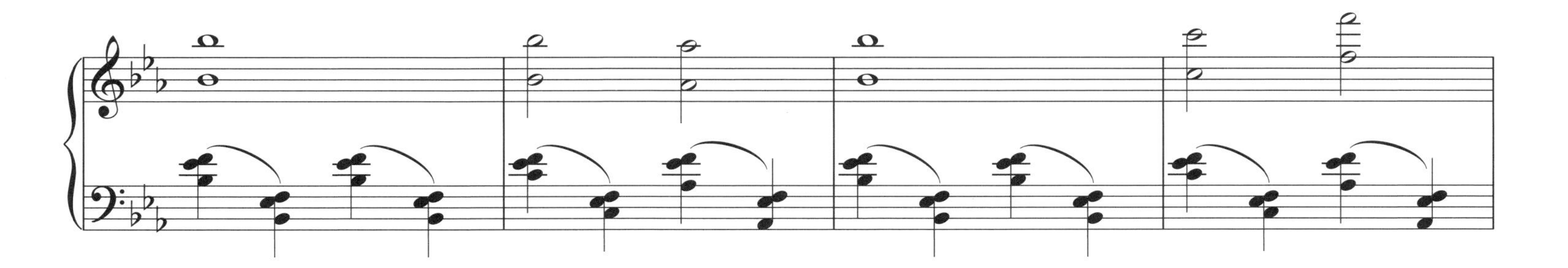

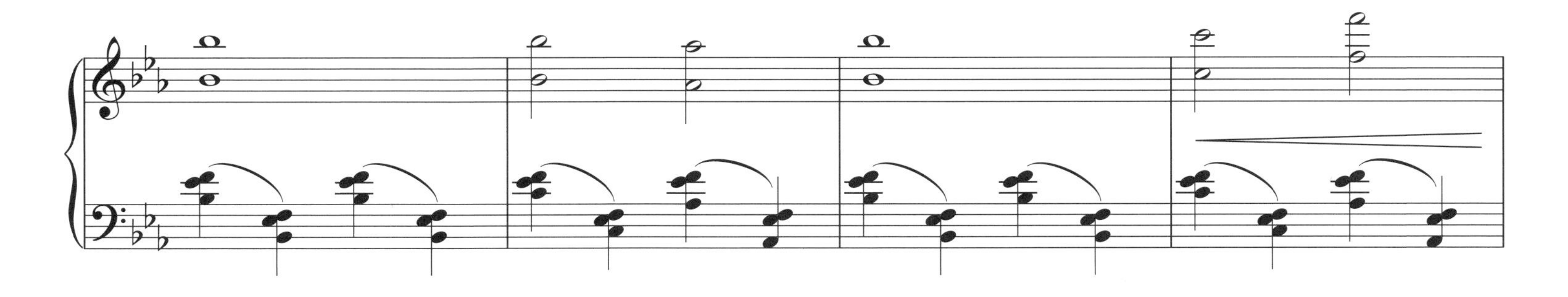

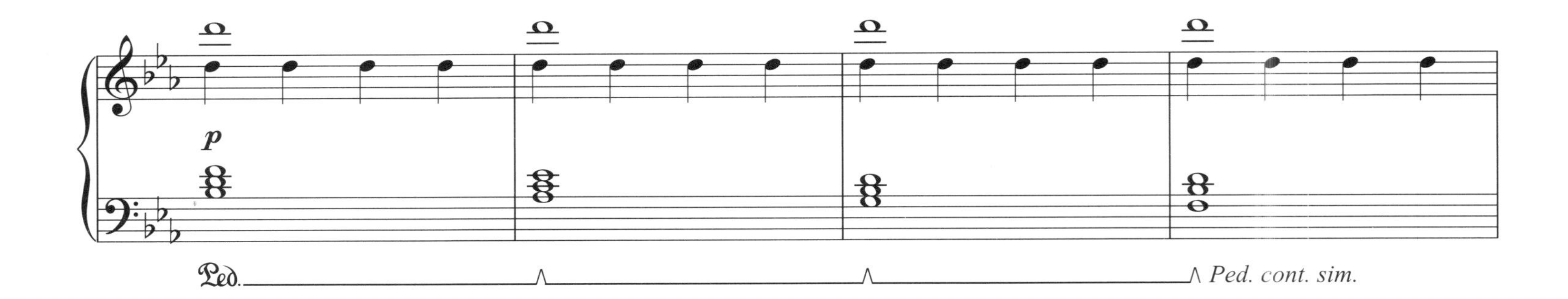
p
Ped.
Ped. cont. sim.

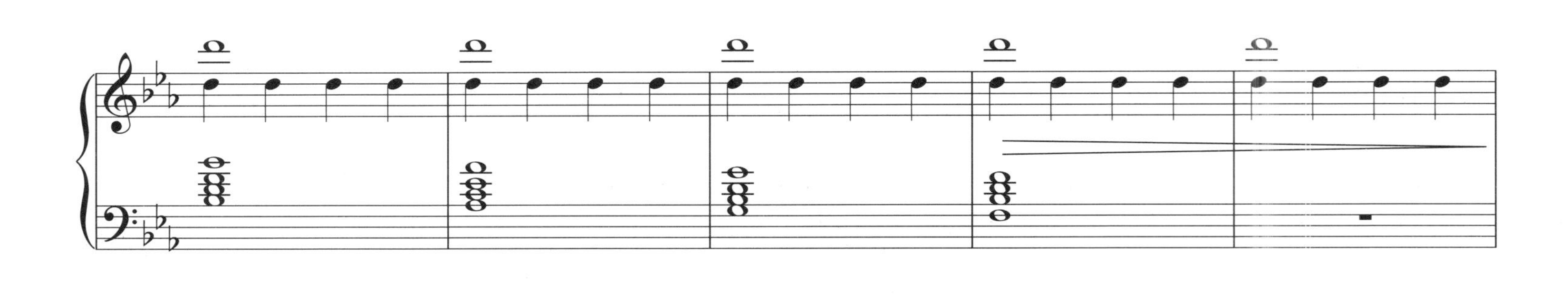

mp
p
Ped.
Ped. cont. sim.

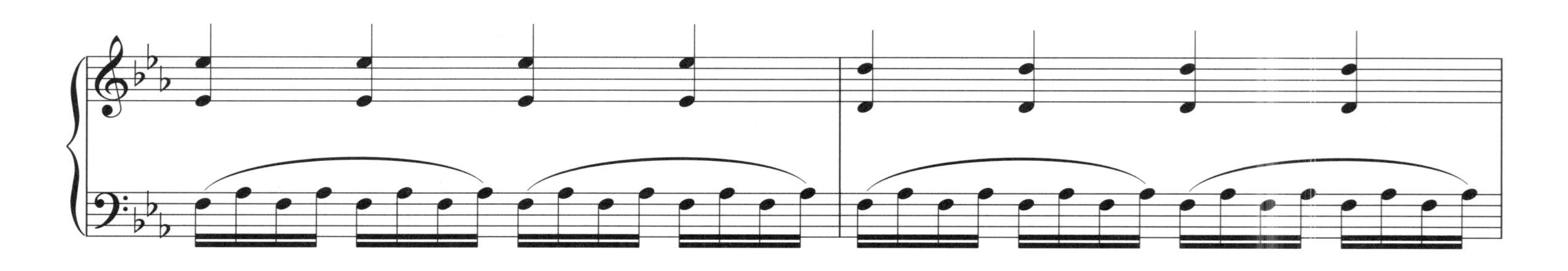

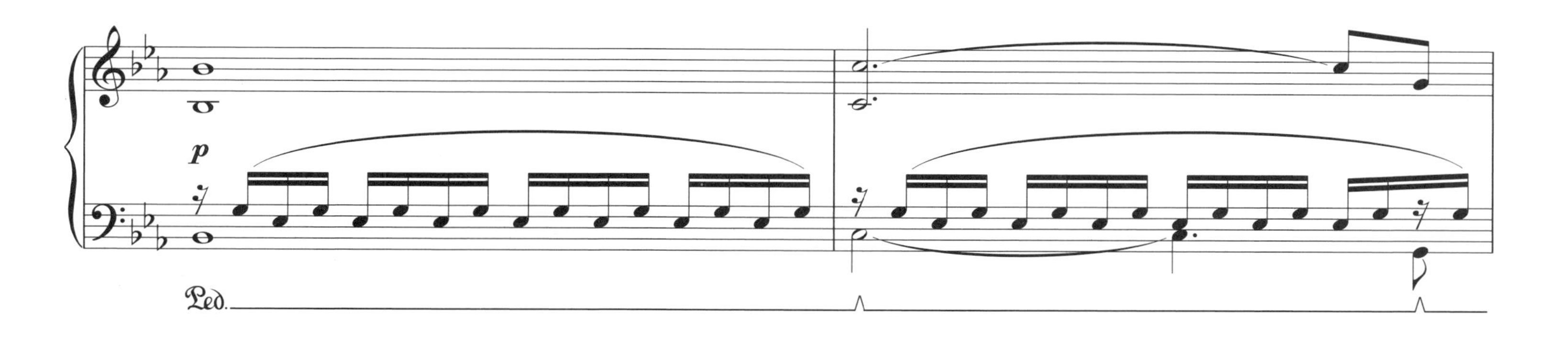
p
Ped.

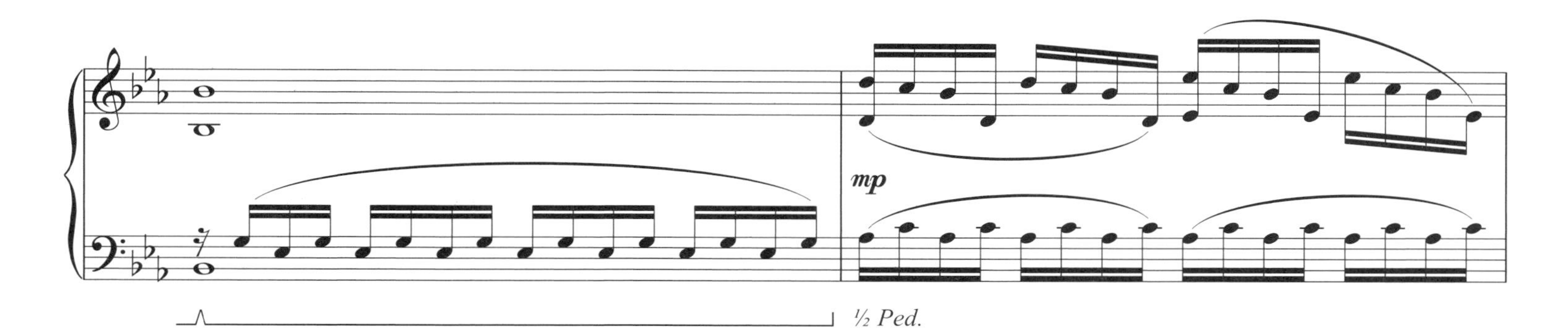
mp
½ Ped.

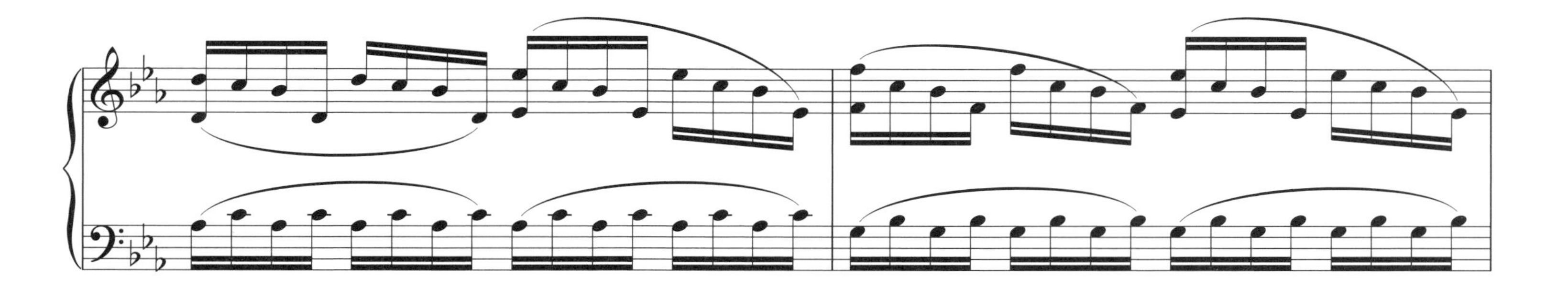

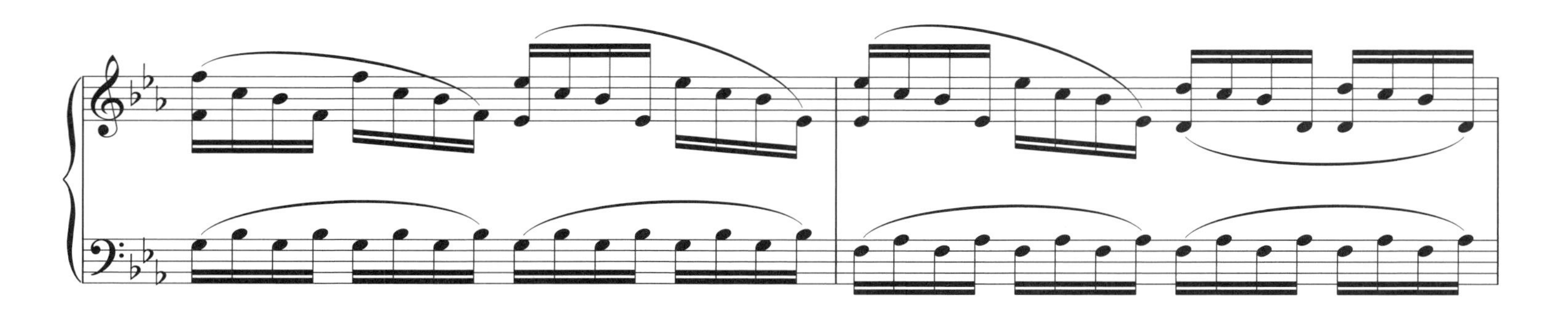

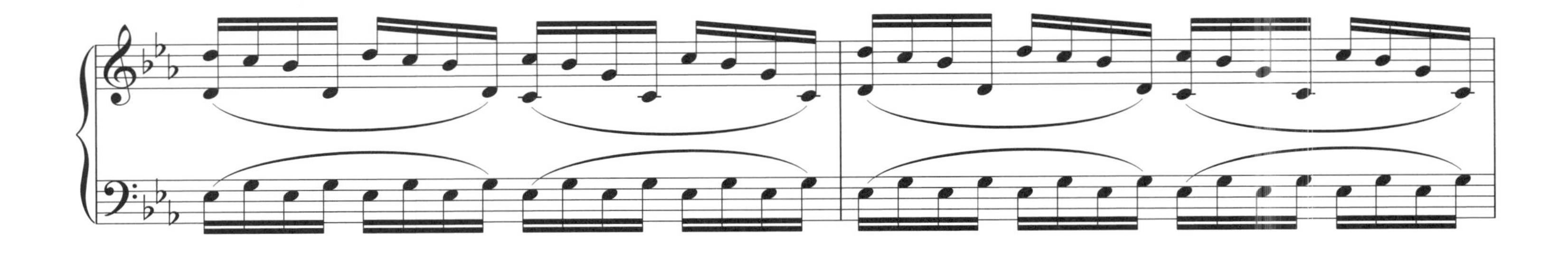

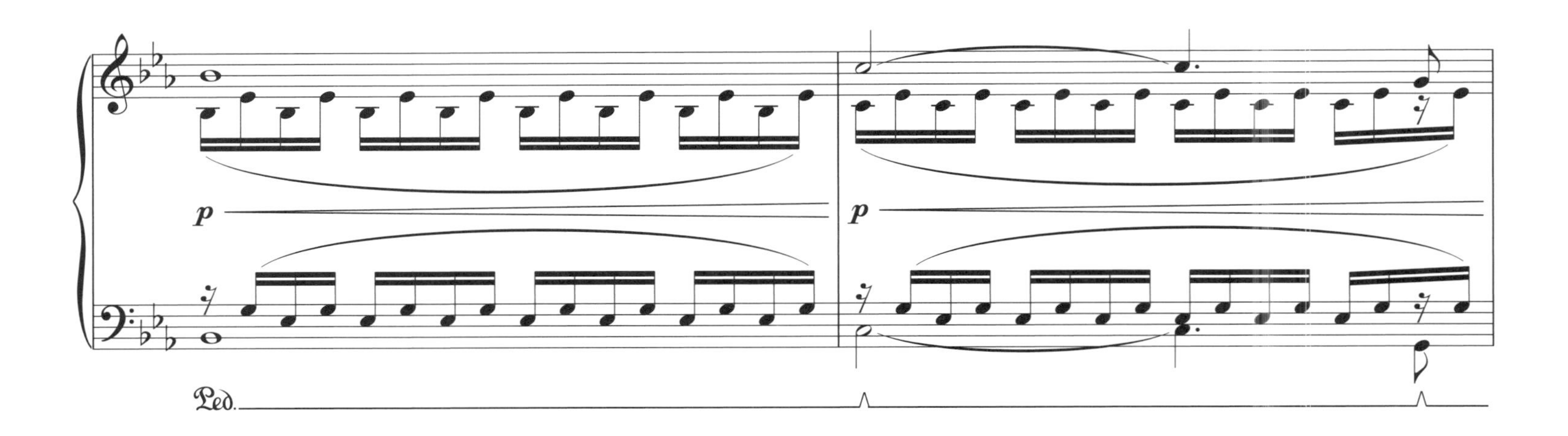

p
p
Ped.

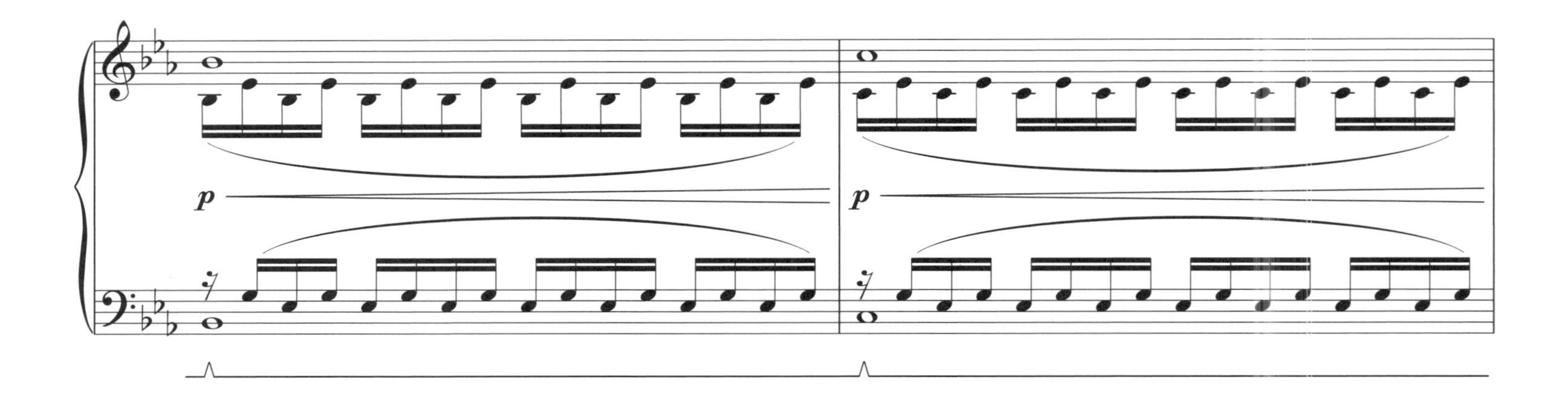

p
p

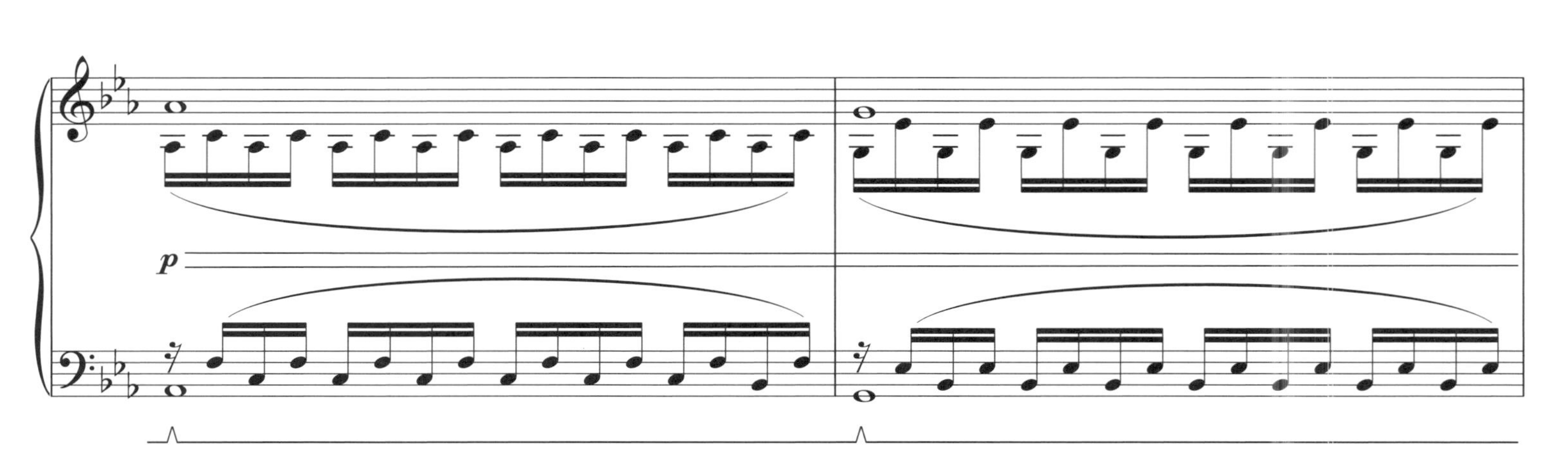

p

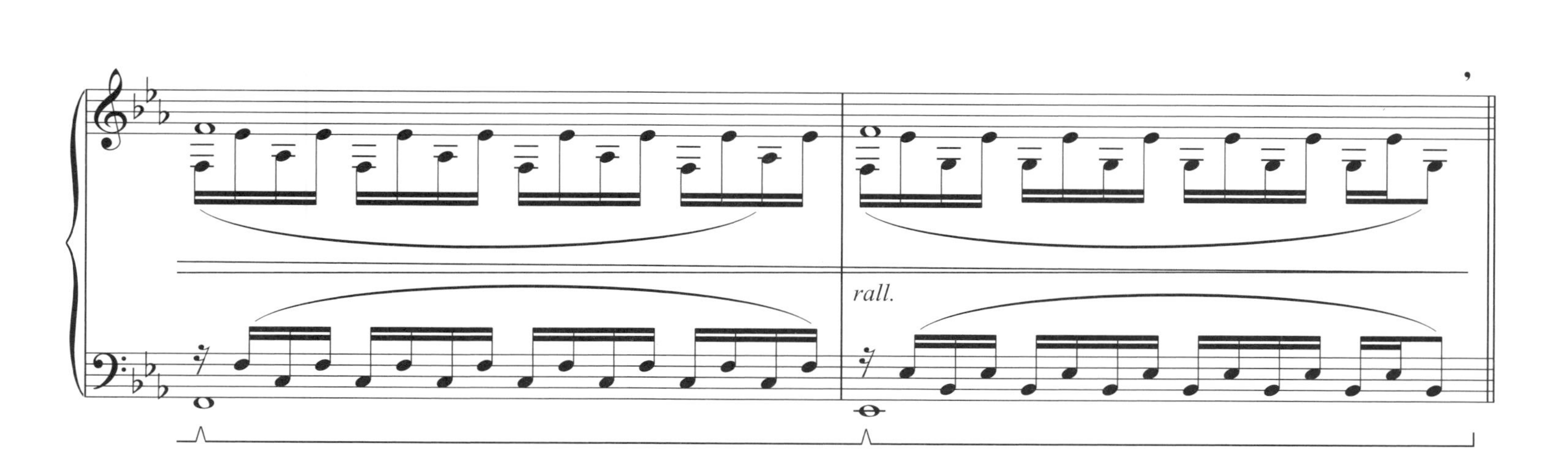
rall.

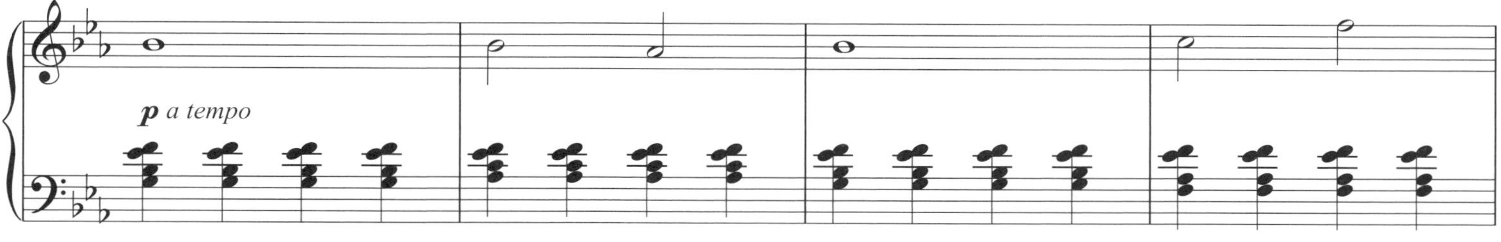
p a tempo
½ Ped.

mp
mp

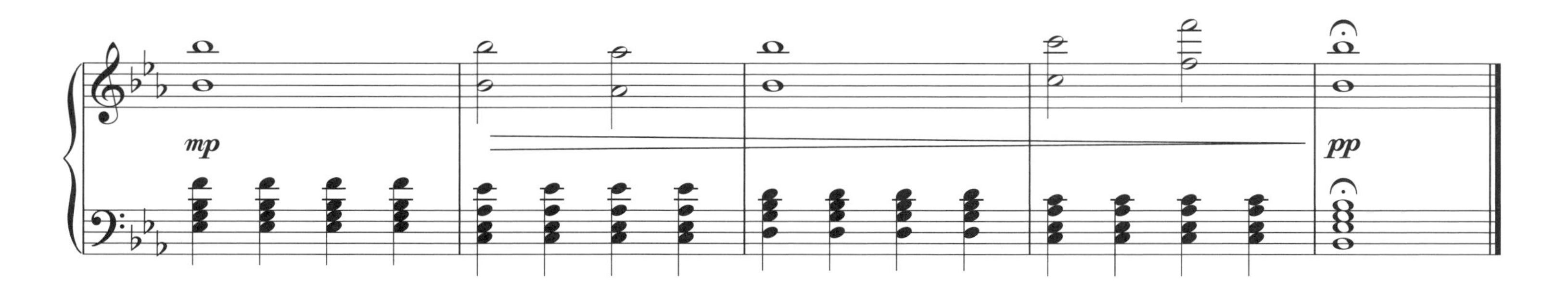
mp
pp

Ar Maner Kozh

MUSIC BY YANN TIERSEN

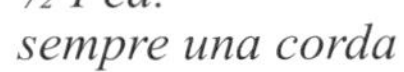

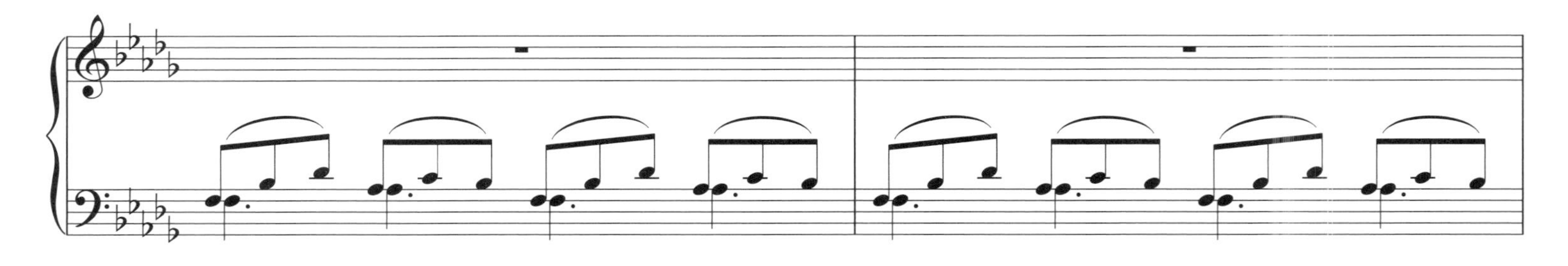

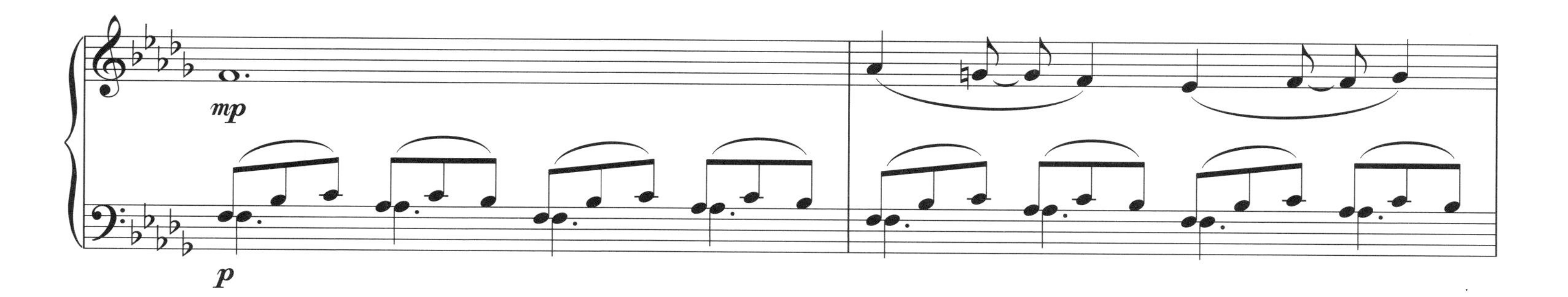
mp
p
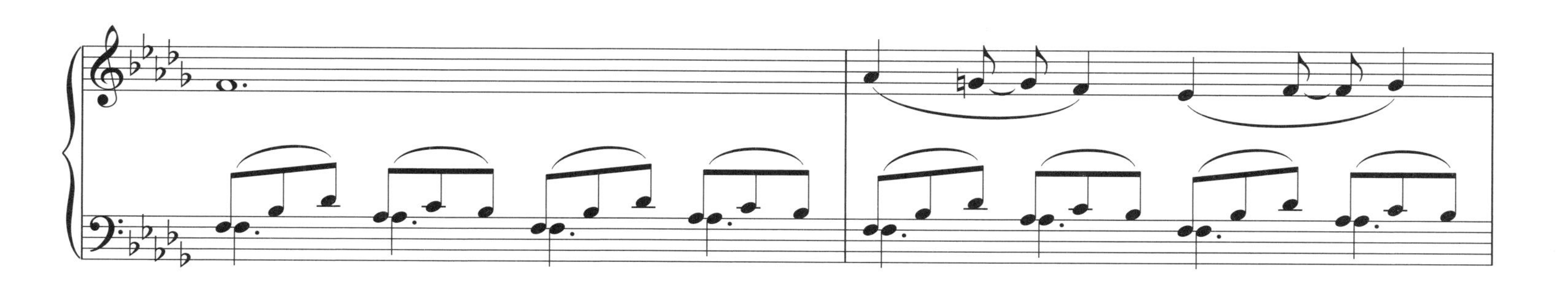
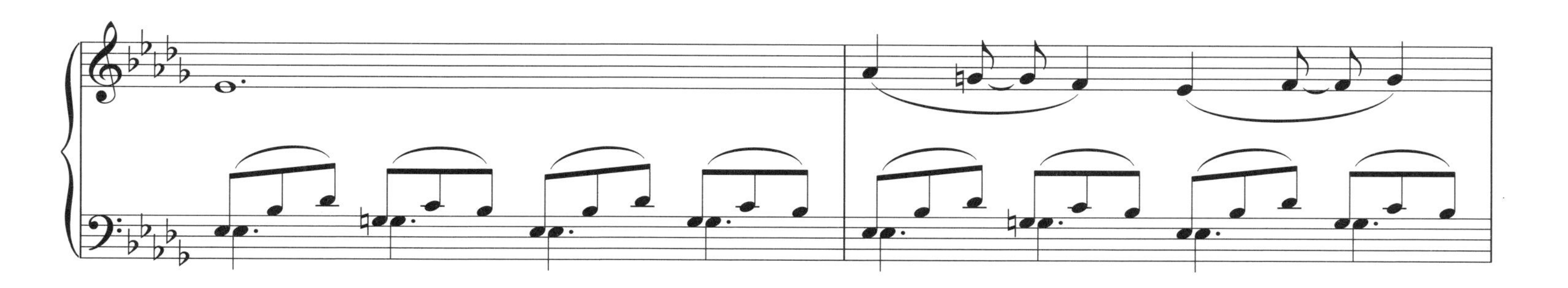
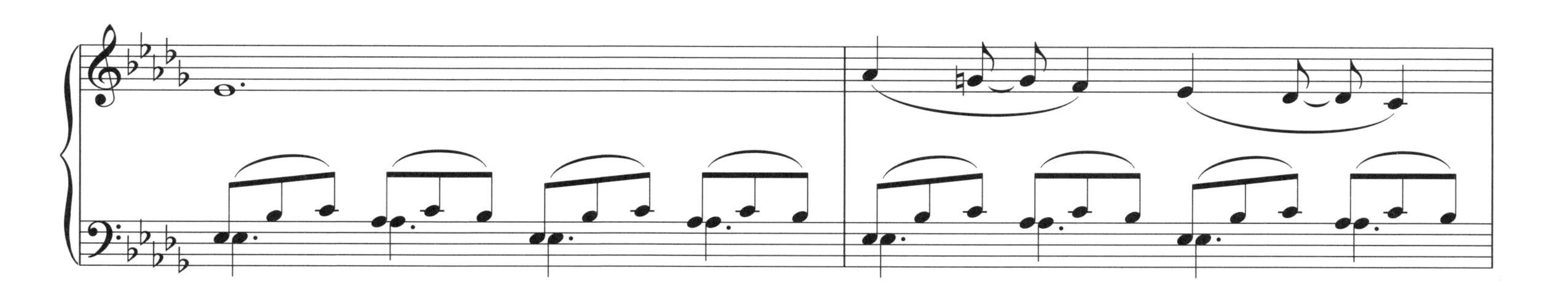

mp

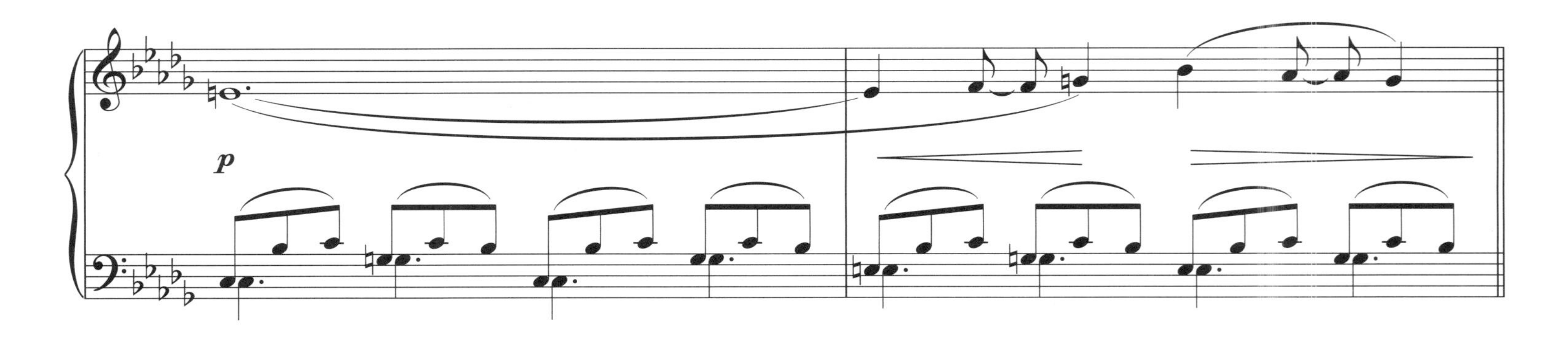
p

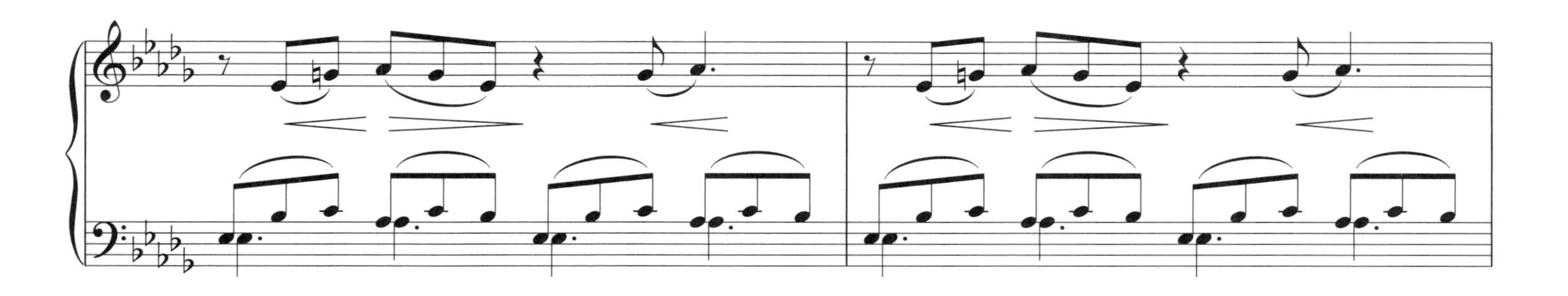

mp
½ Ped.

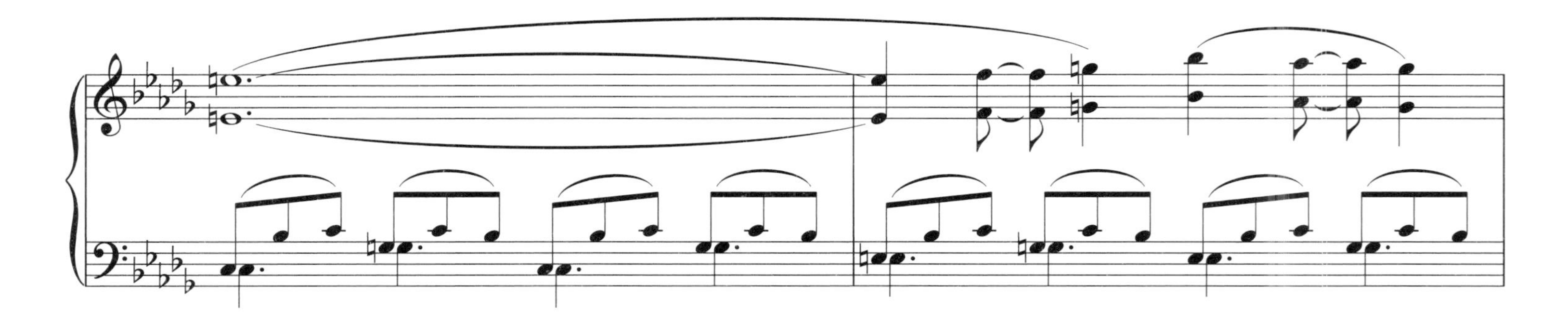

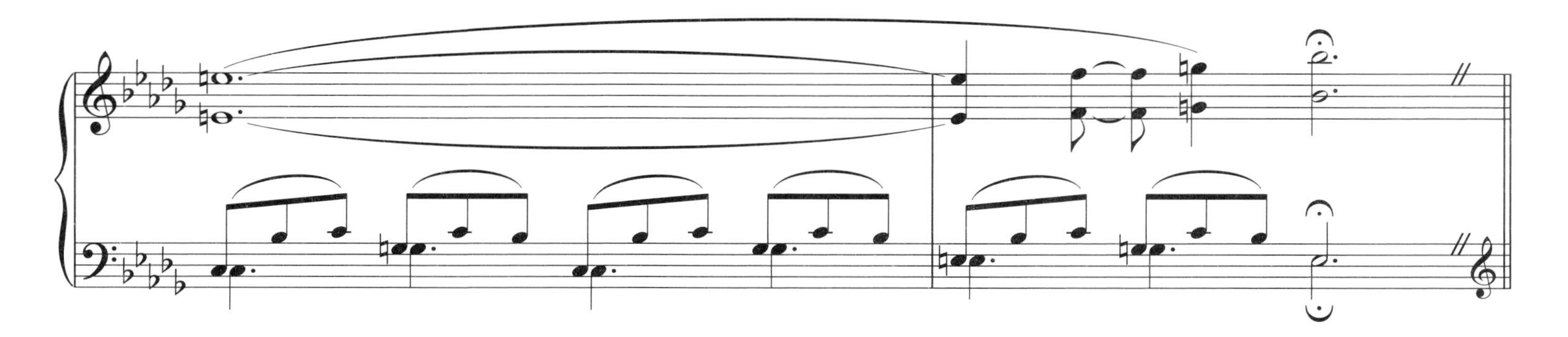

p

rall.

Kerdrall

MUSIC BY YANN TIERSEN

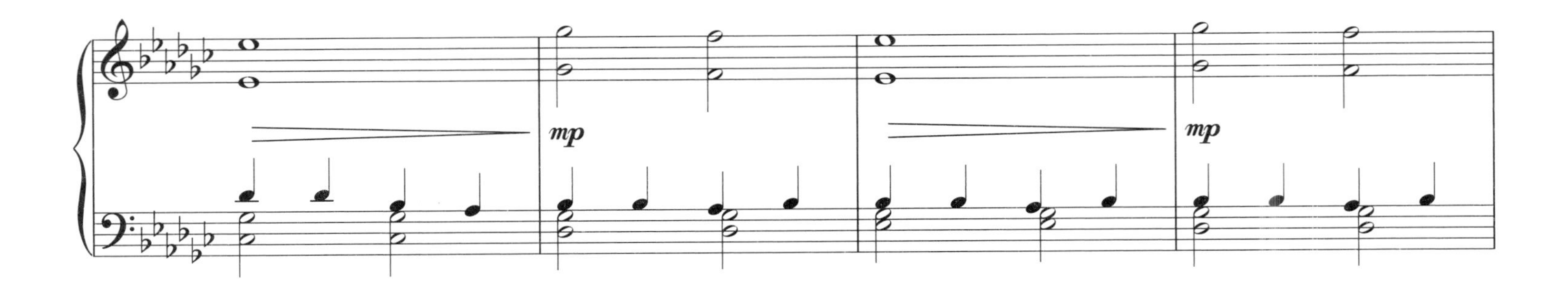
mp
mp

mp
p

pp
8vb
Ped.
Ped. cont. sim.

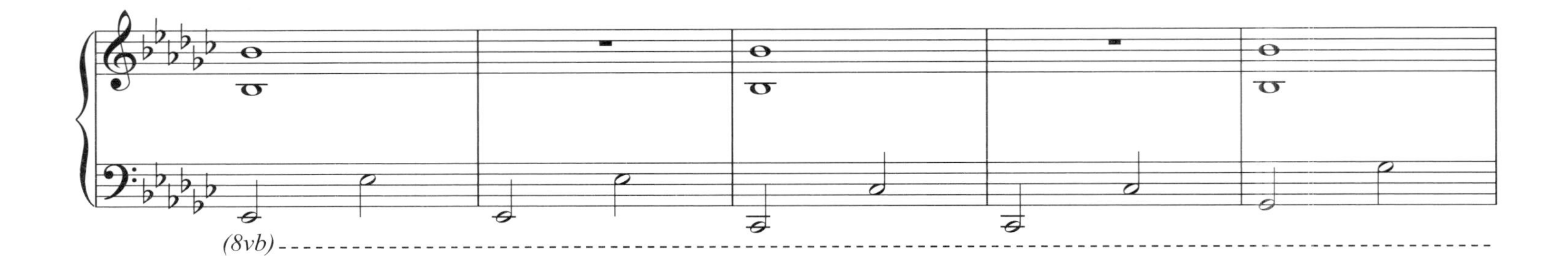
(8vb)

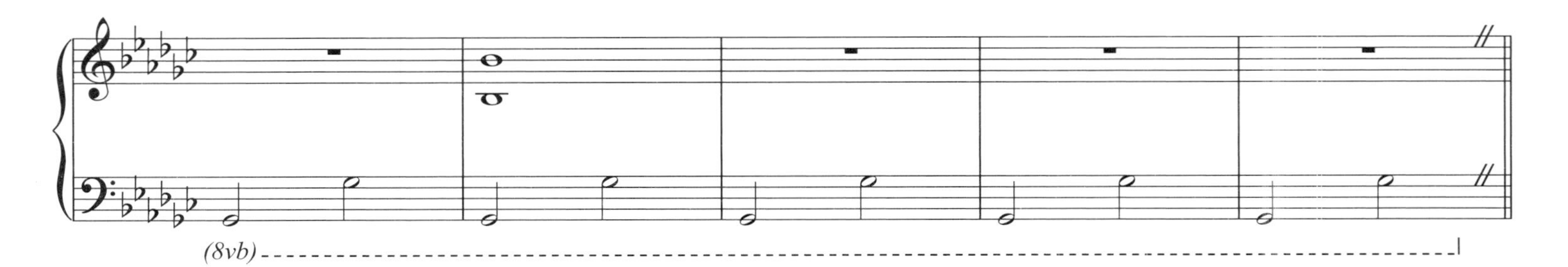
(8vb)

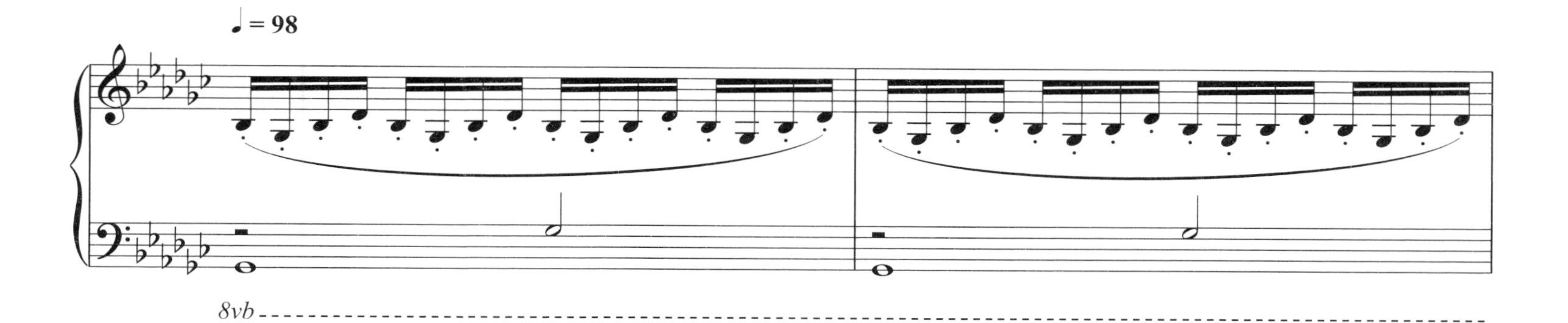
♩ = 98
8vb

(8vb)
½ Ped.
Ped.
Ped. cont. sim.

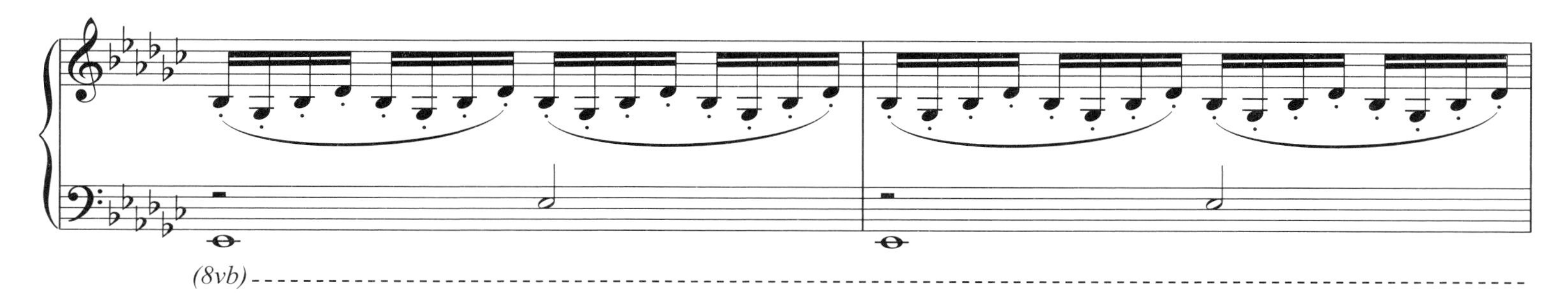
(8vb)

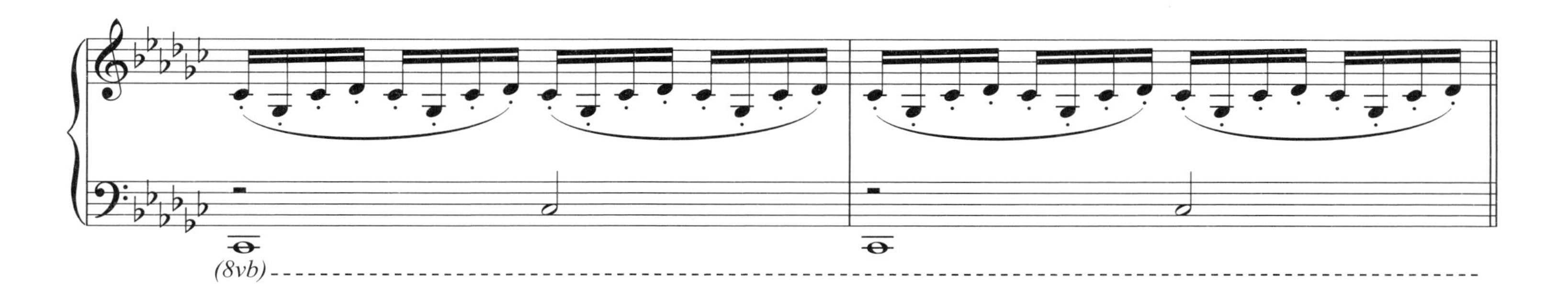
(8vb)

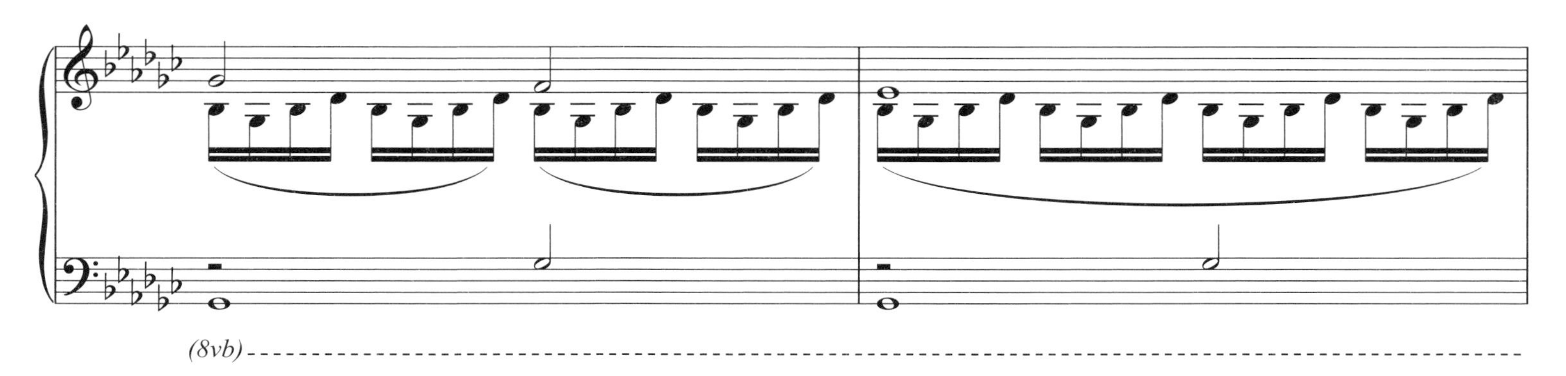
(8vb)

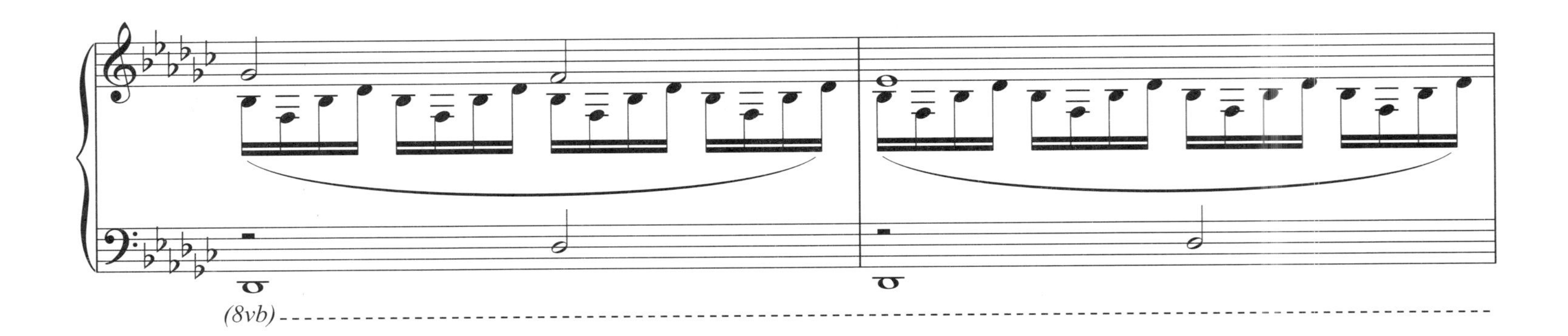
(8vb)

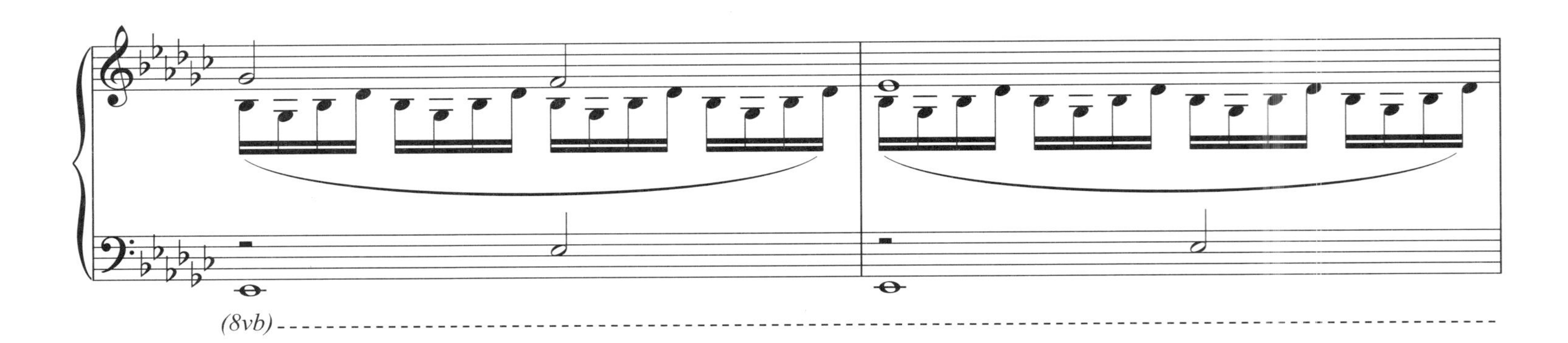
(8vb)

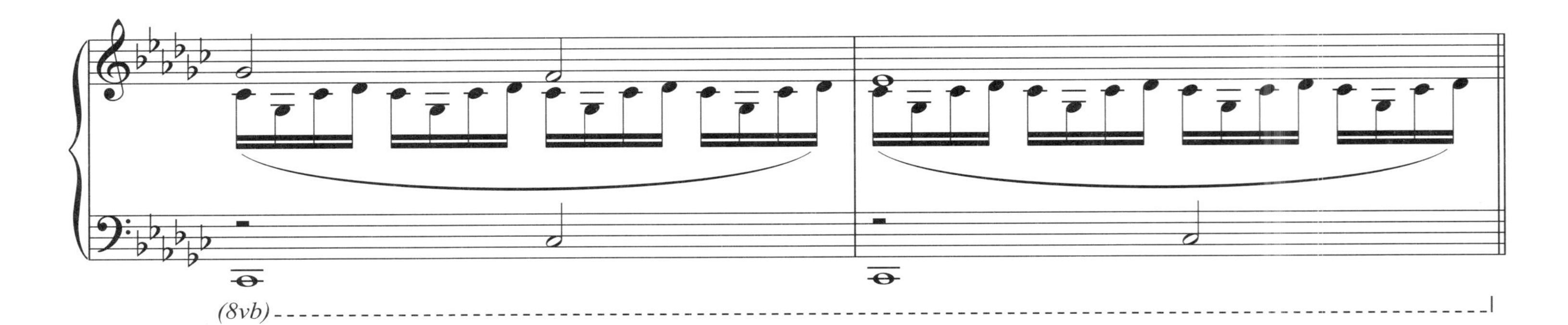
(8vb)

mp
Ped.
Ped. cont. sim.

mf
Ped.
Ped. cont. sim.
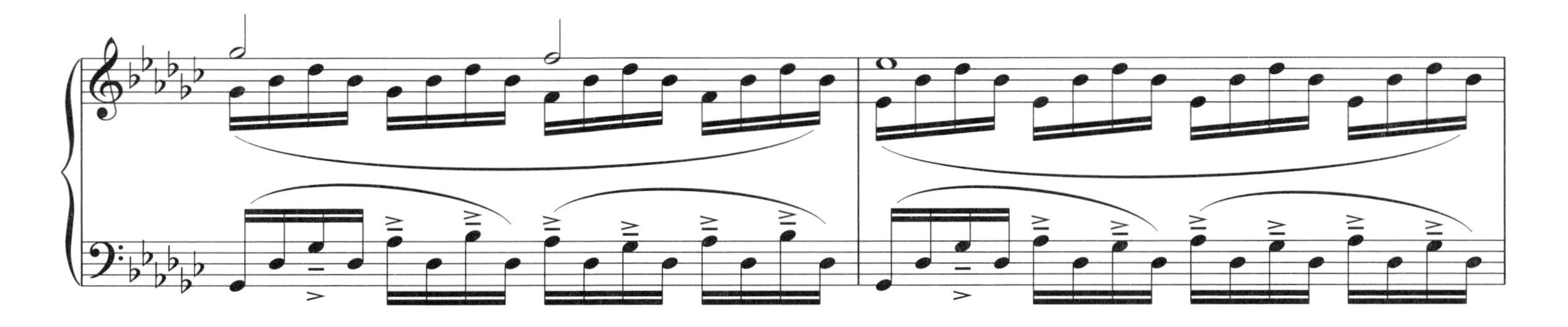

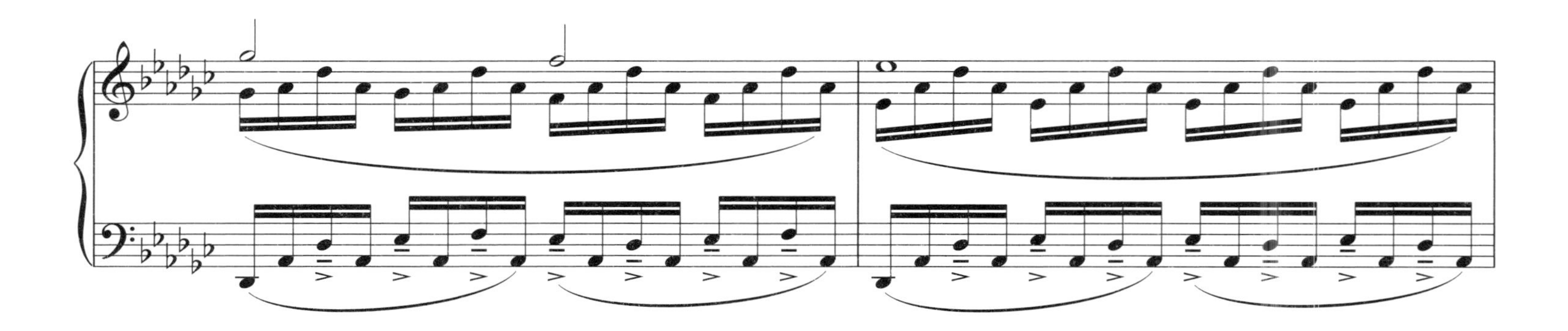

rall.

♩ = 68
p a tempo

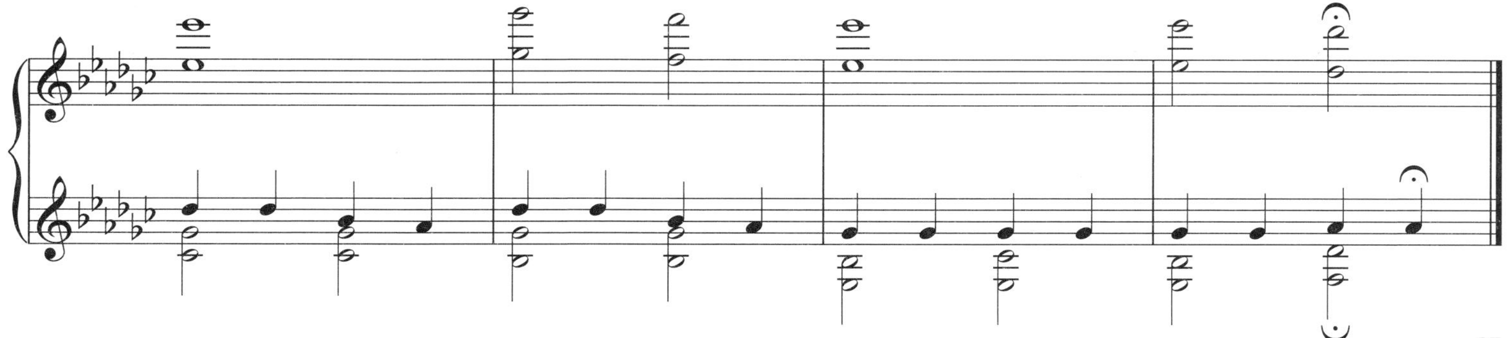

Ker Yegu

MUSIC BY YANN TIERSEN

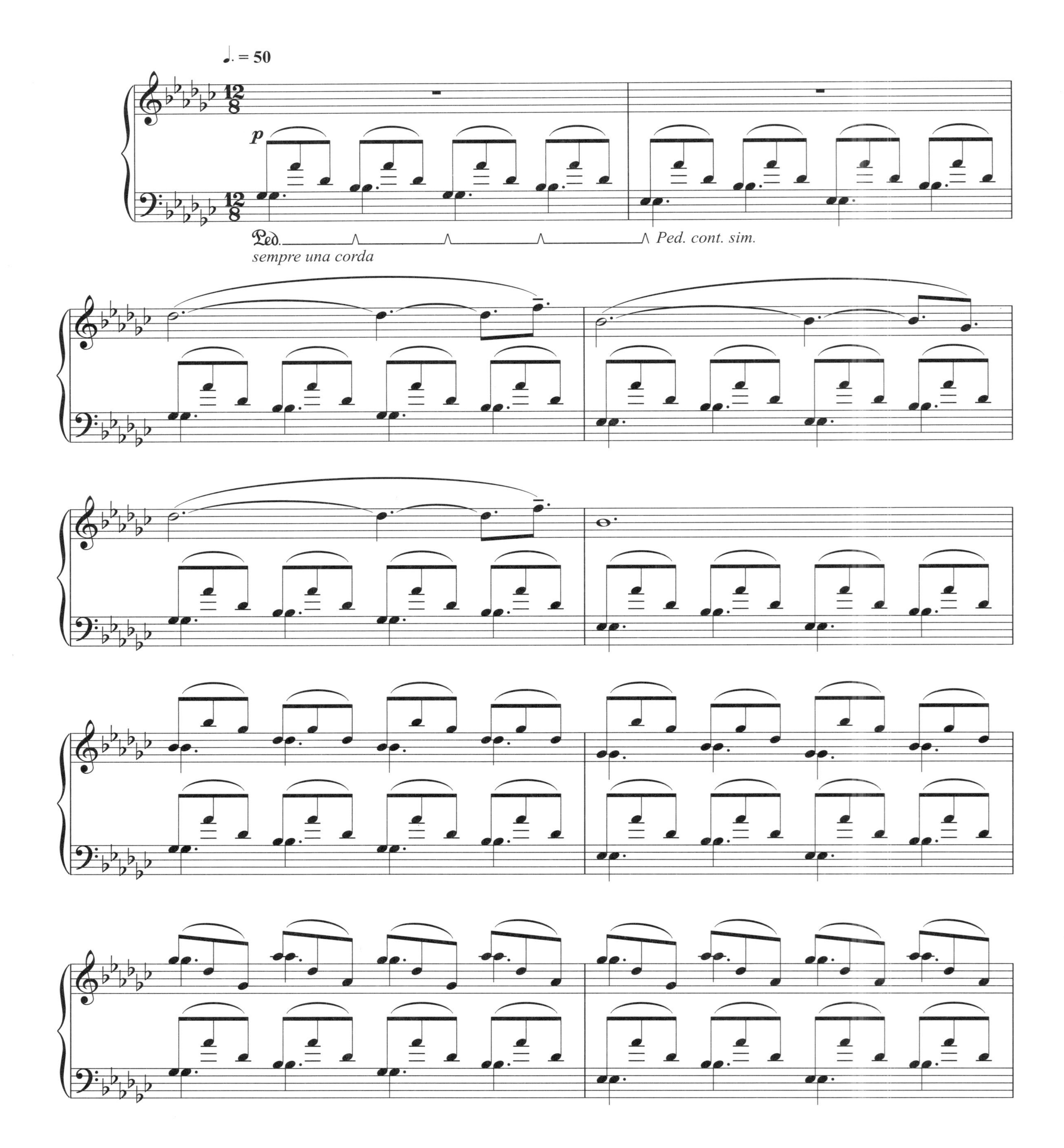

mp

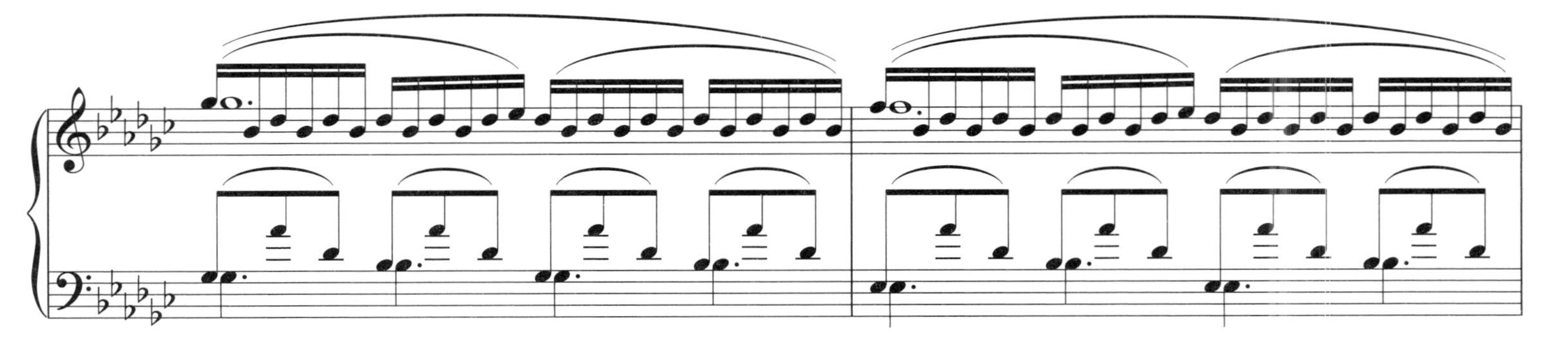

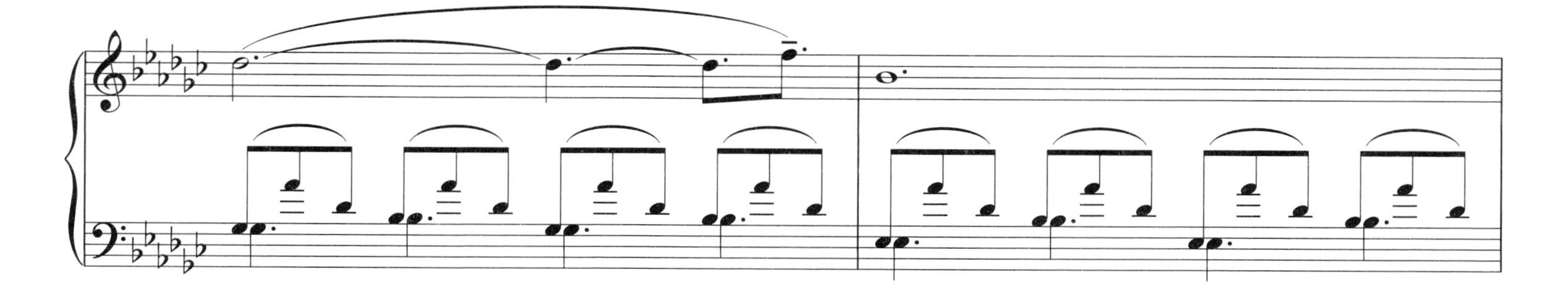

8va

(8va)

Ker al Loch

MUSIC BY YANN TIERSEN

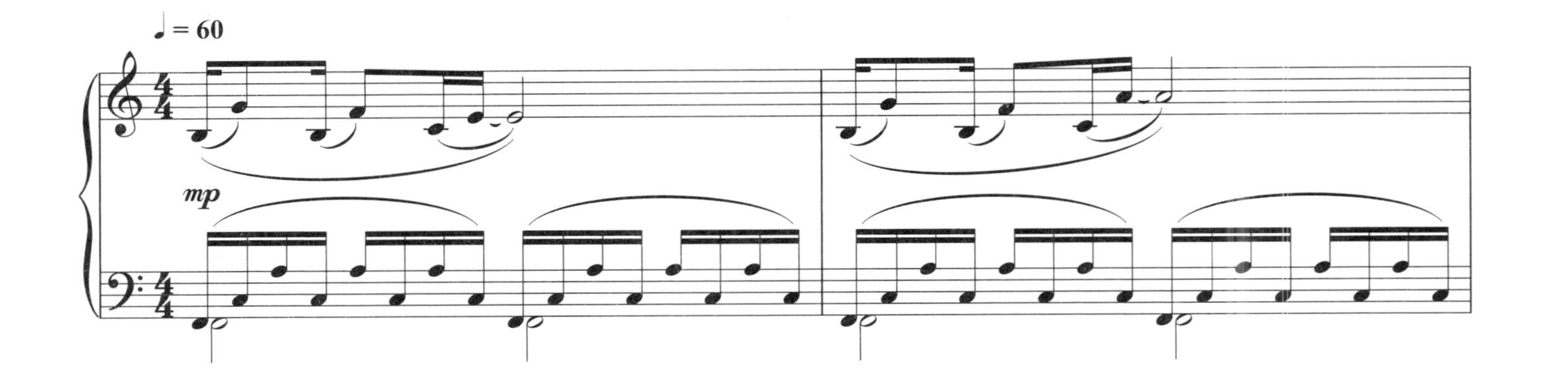

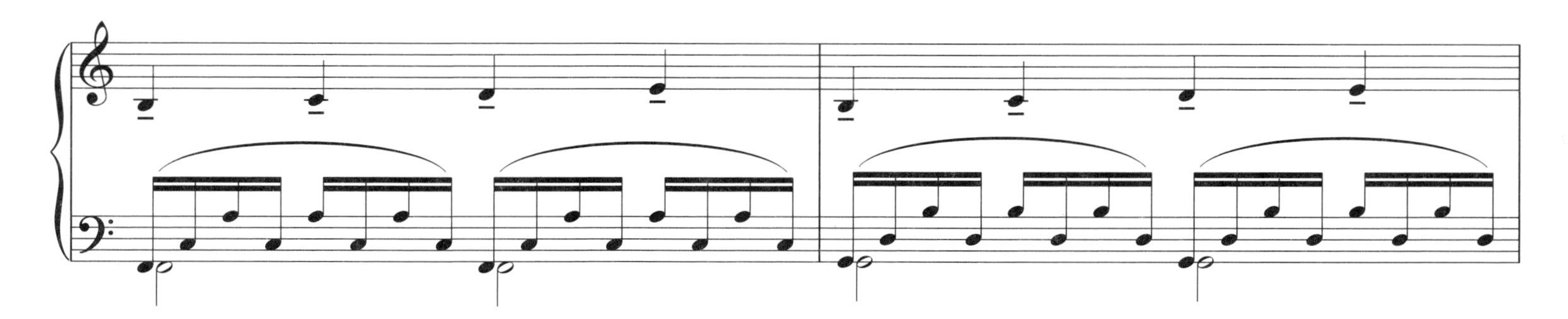

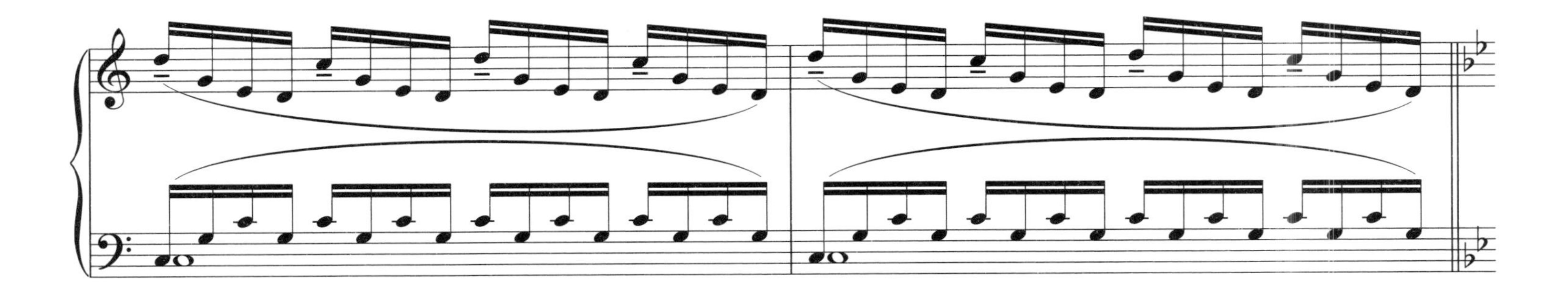

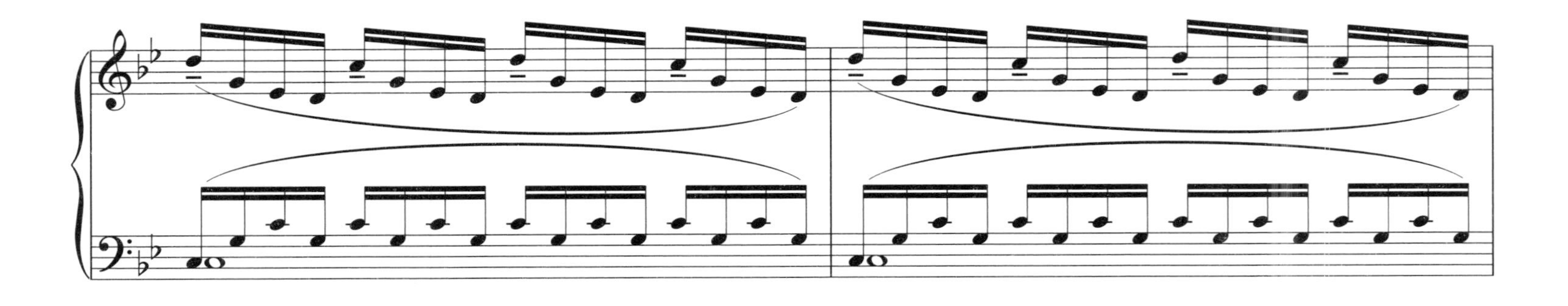

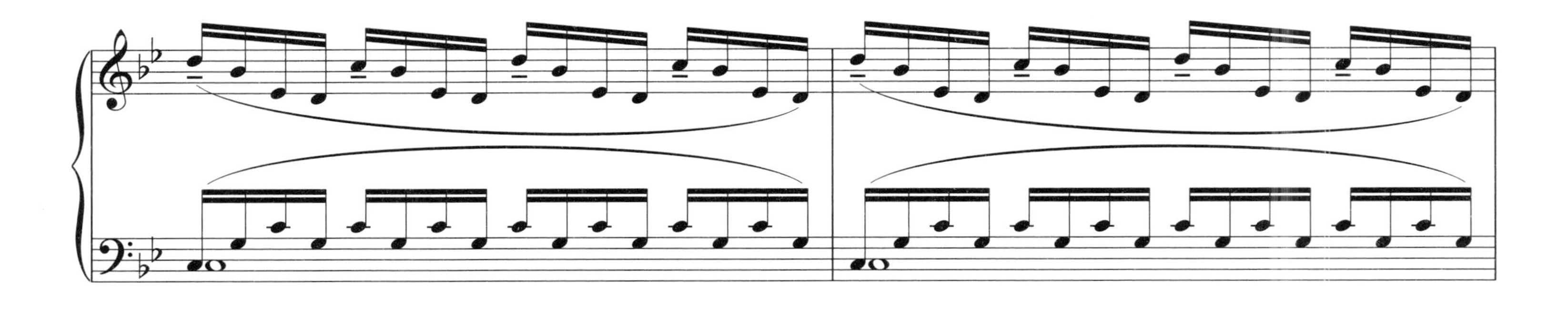

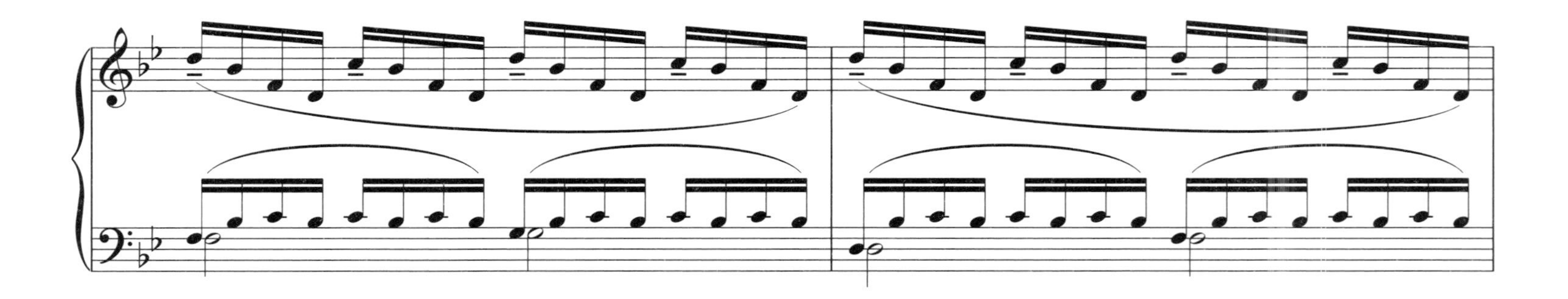

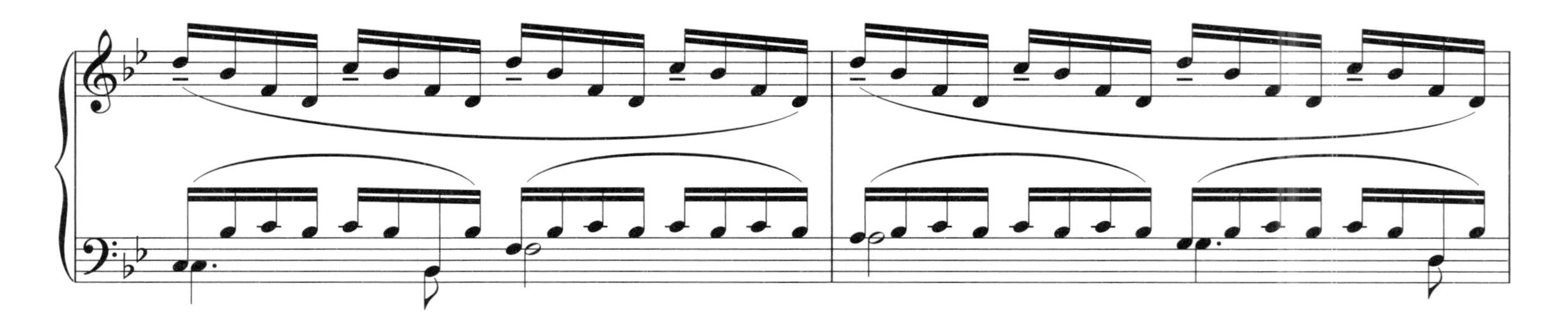

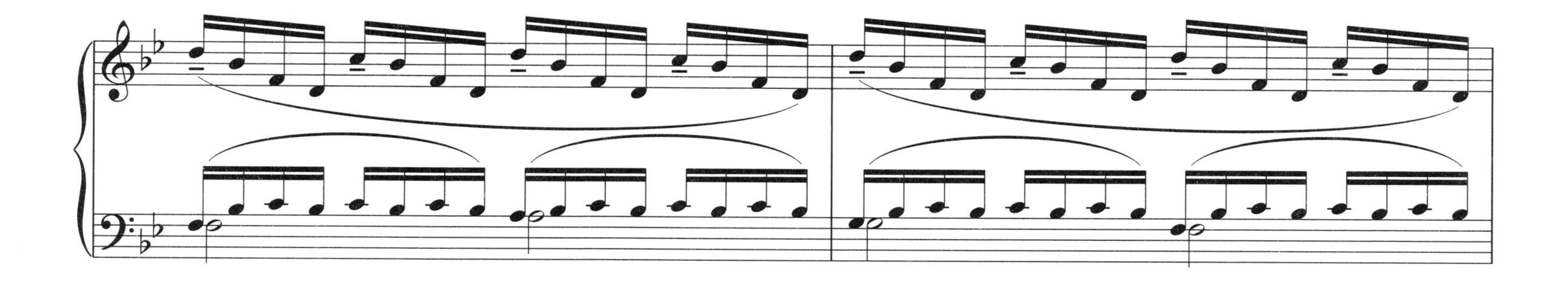

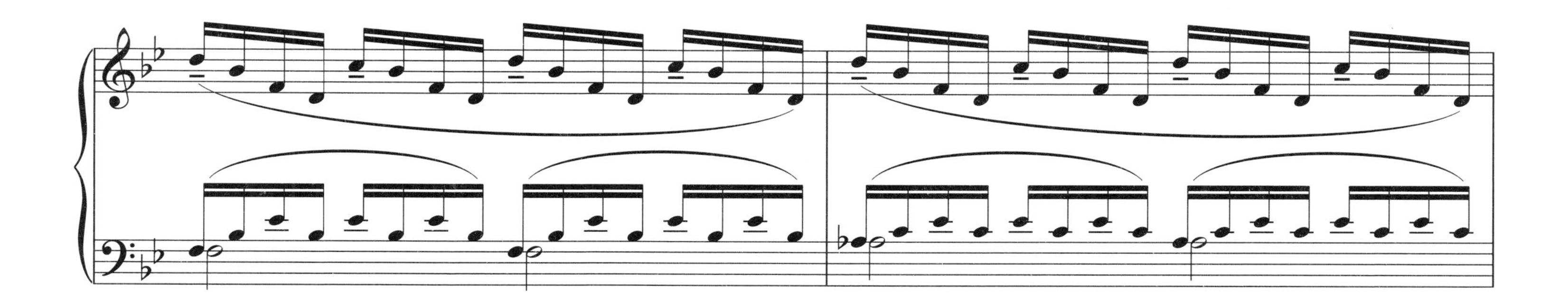

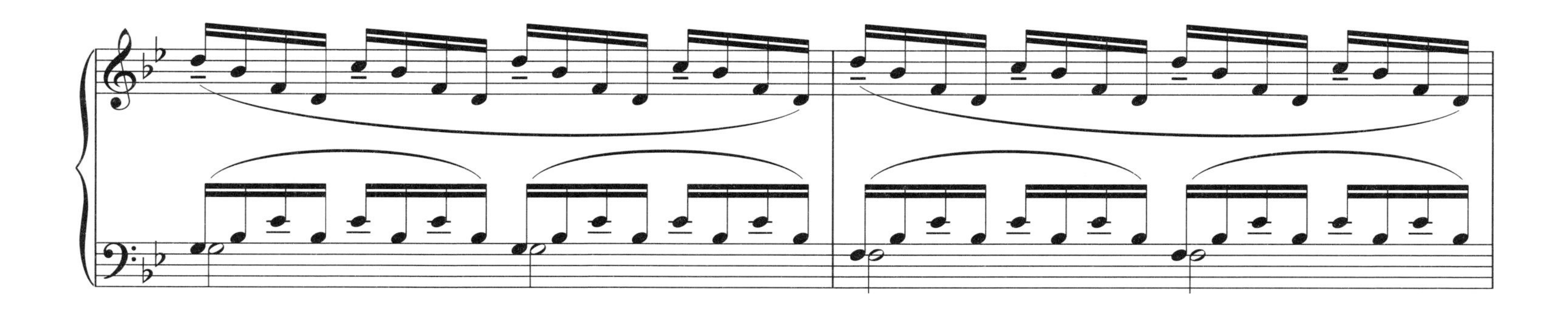

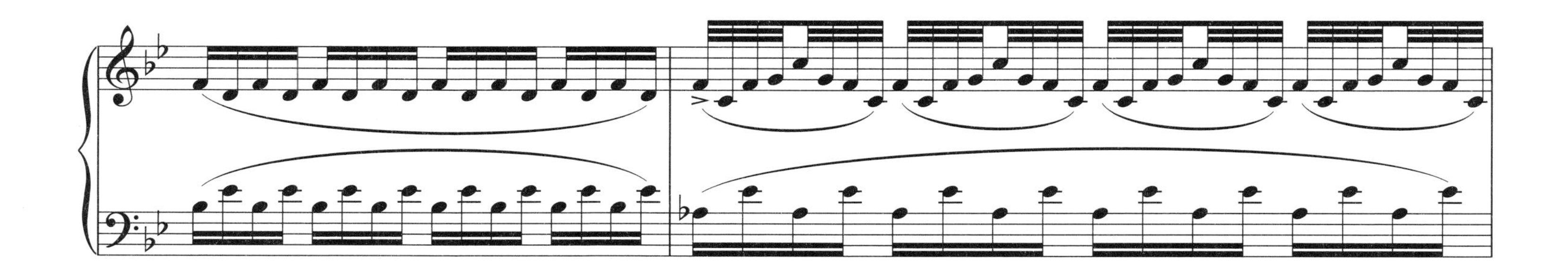

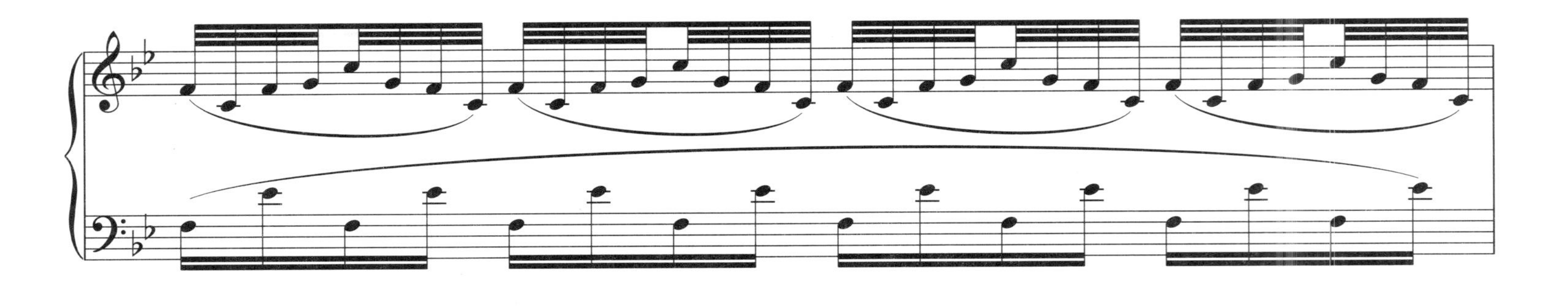

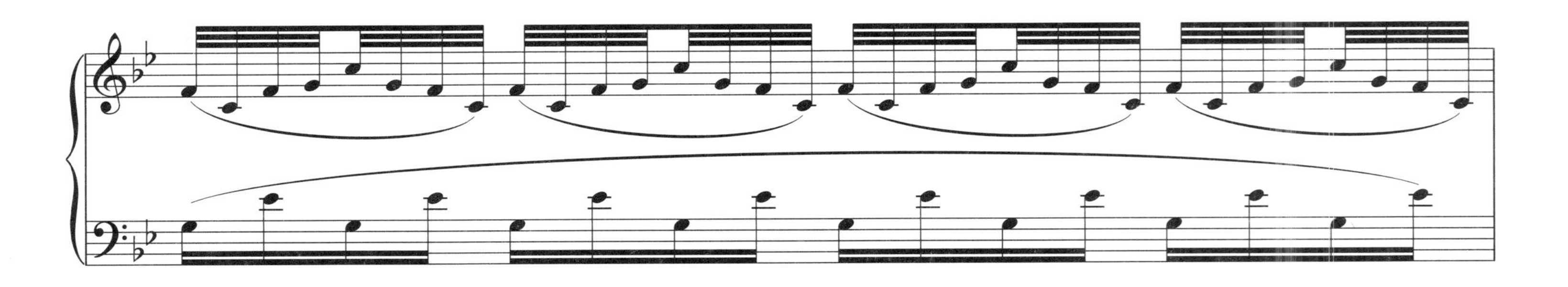

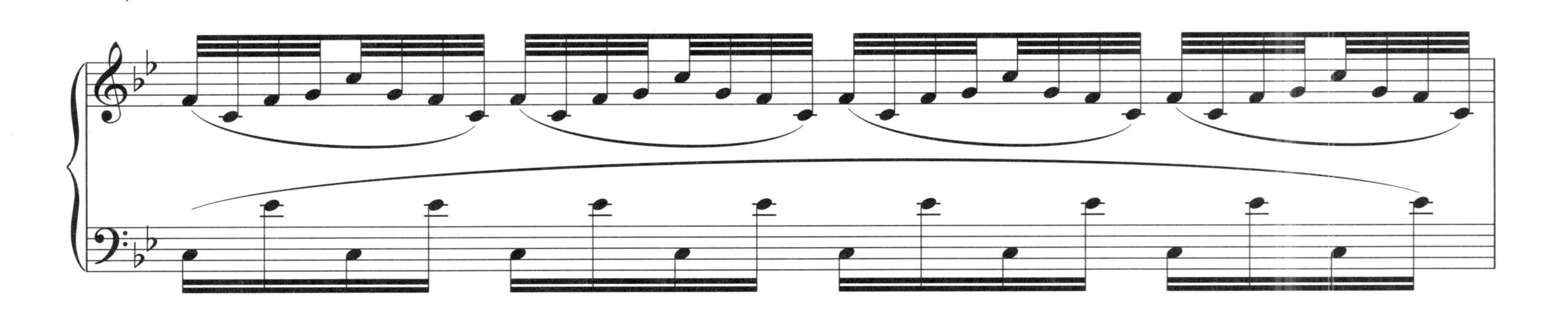

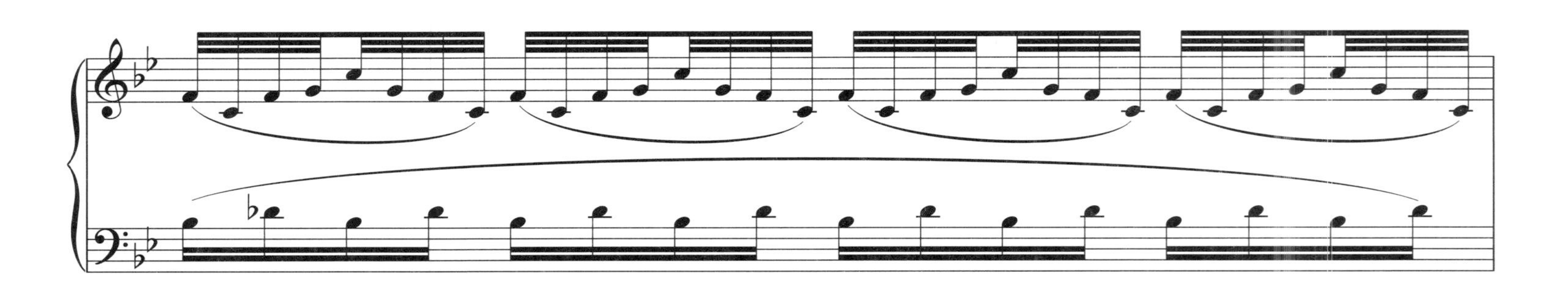

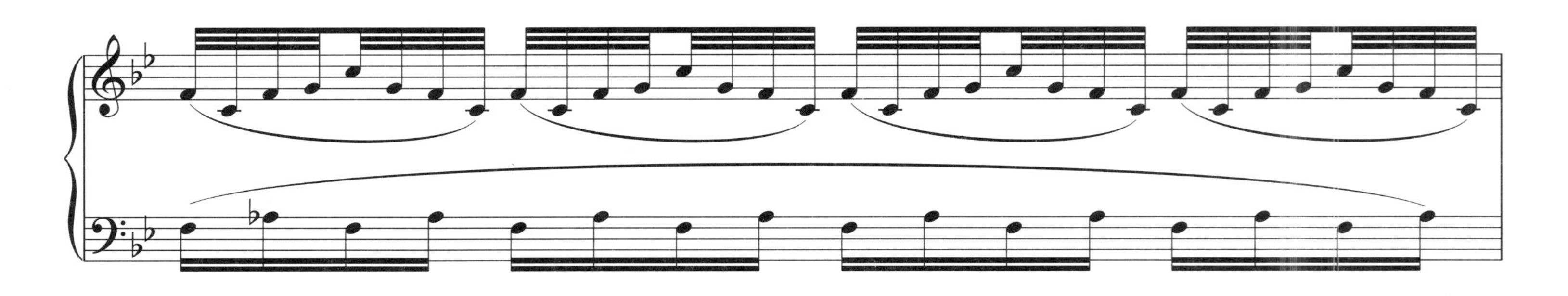

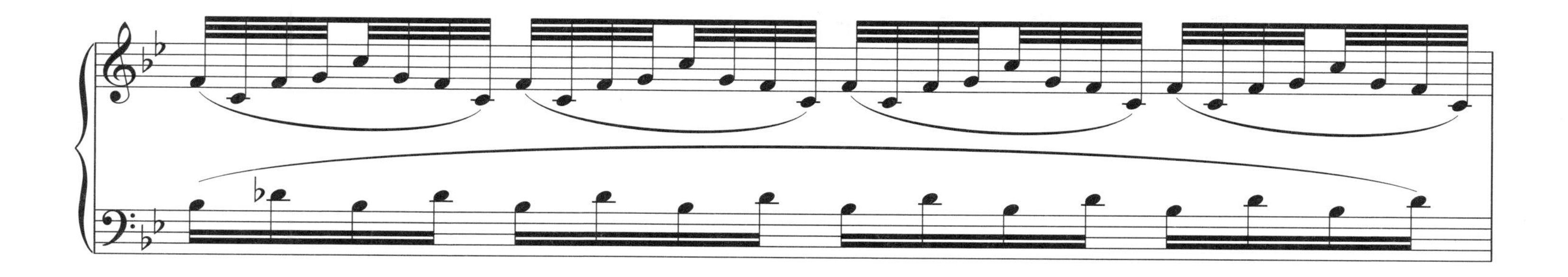

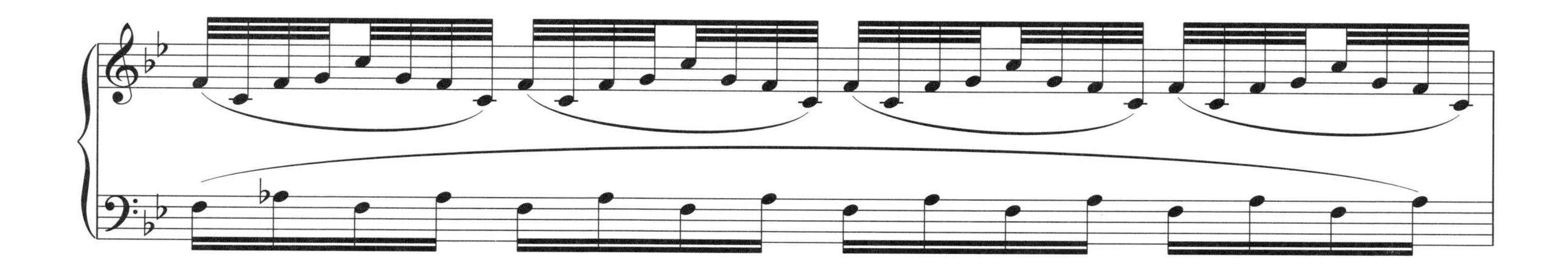

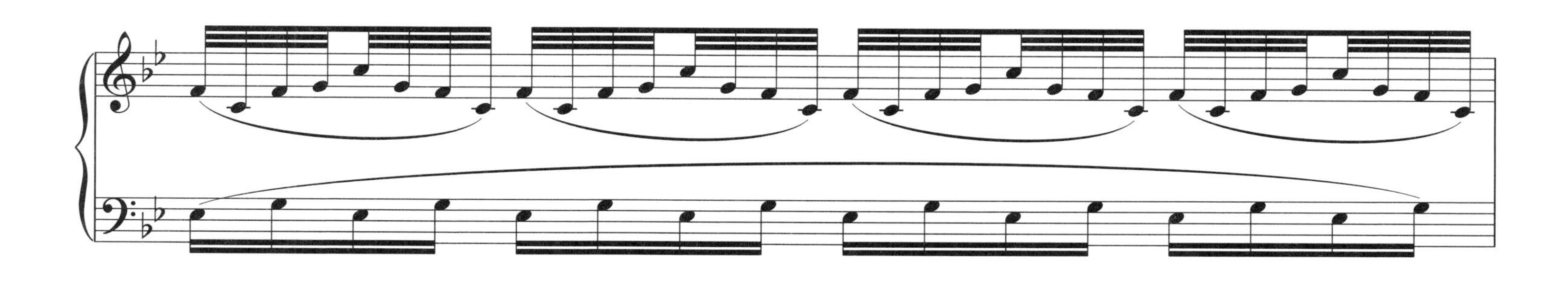

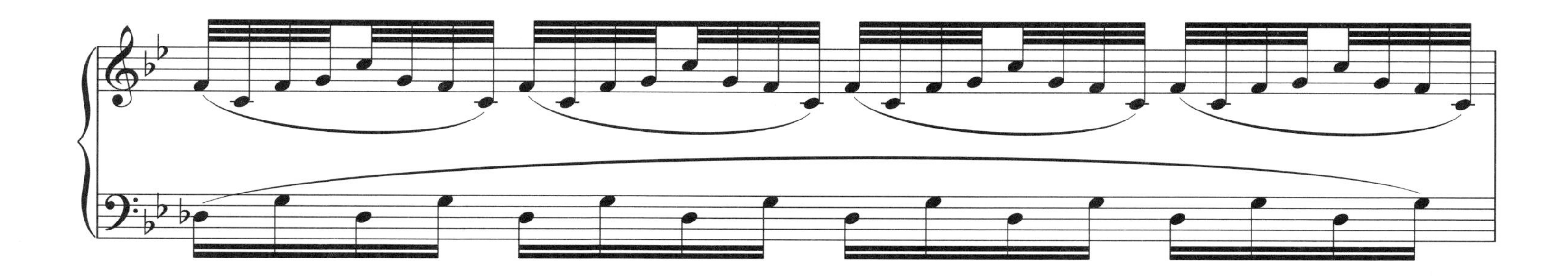

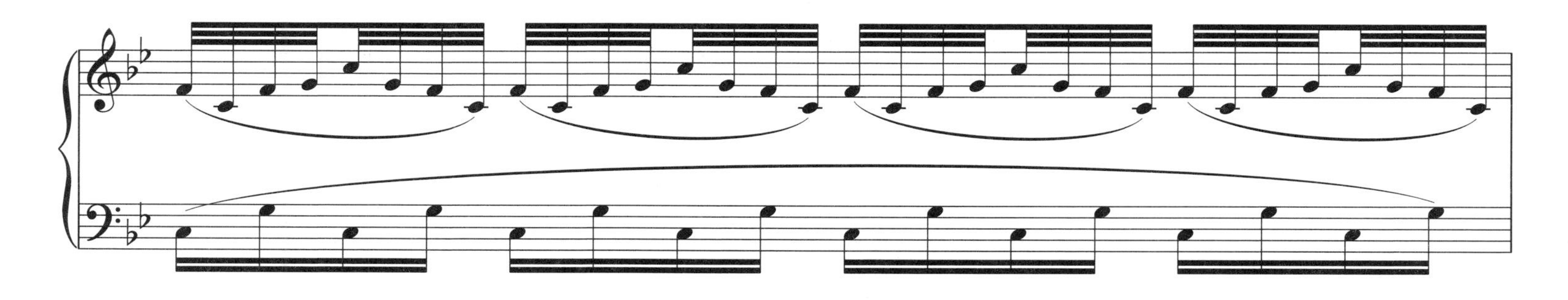

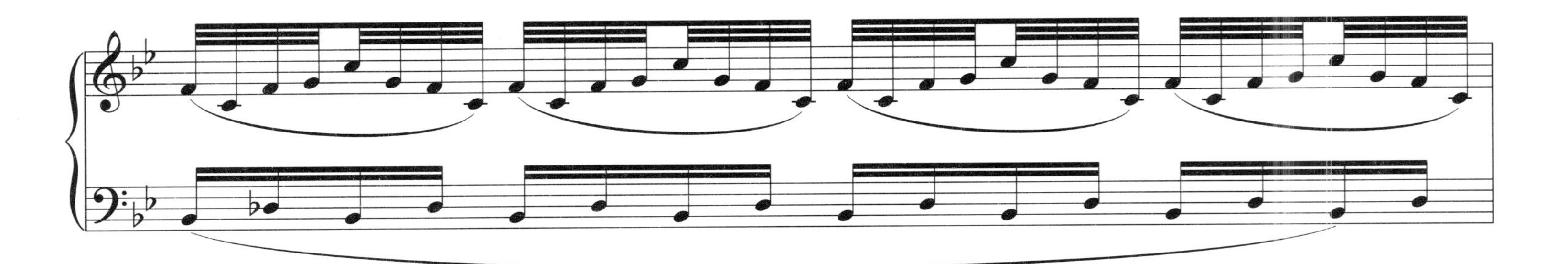

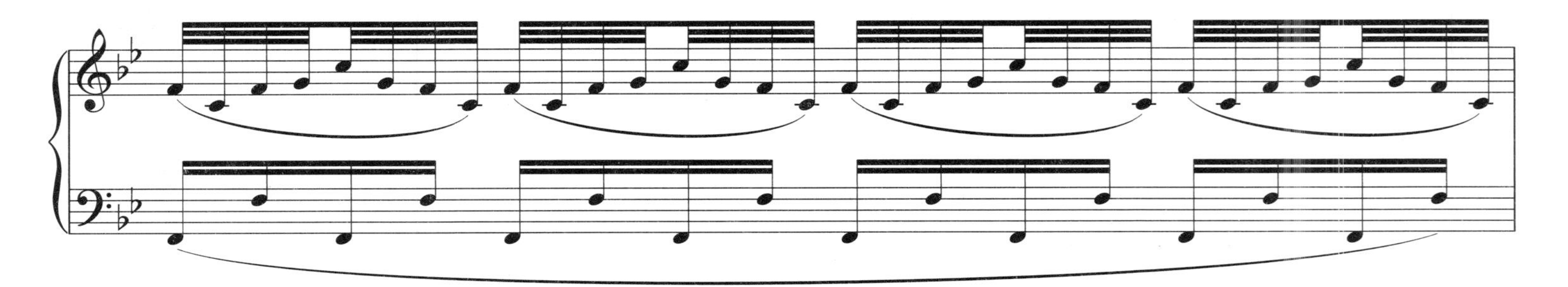

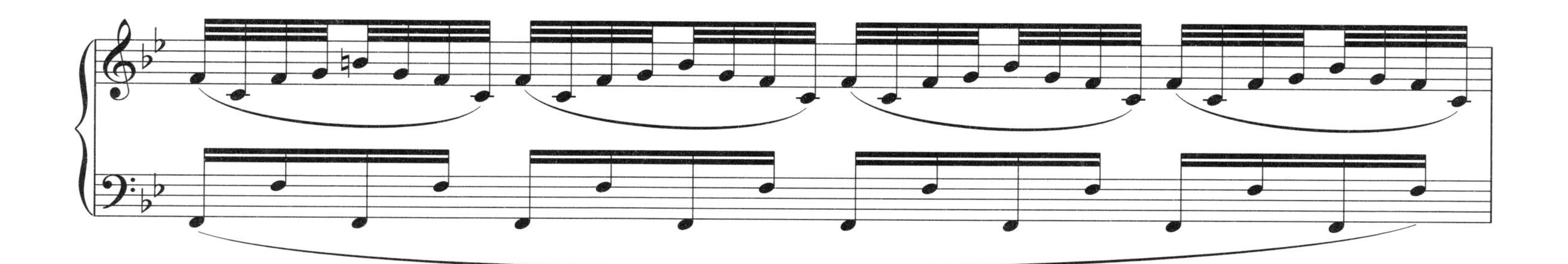

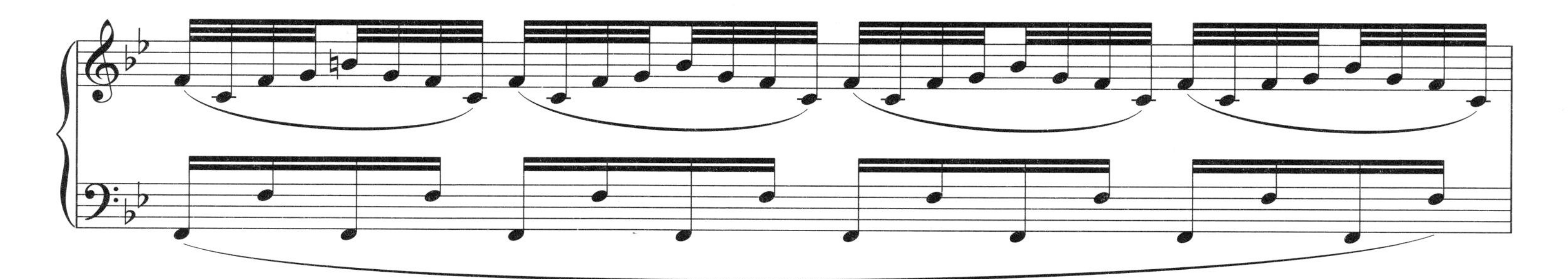

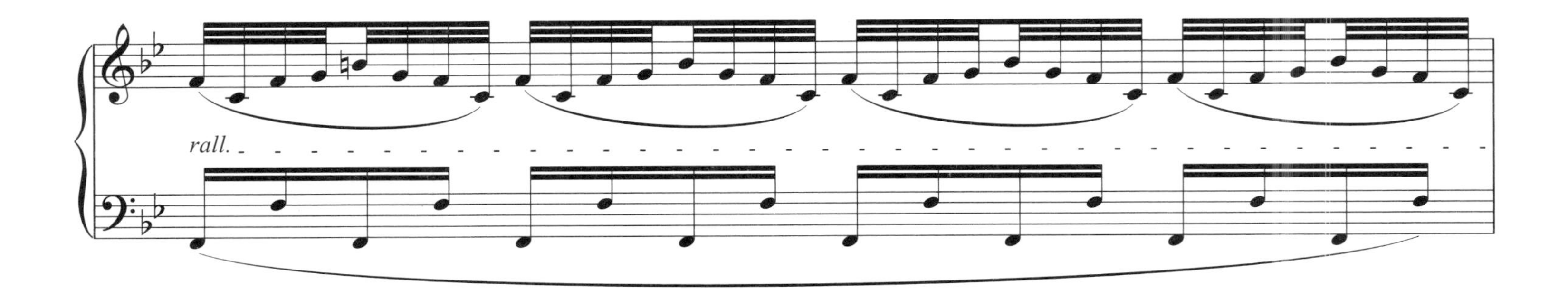
rall.

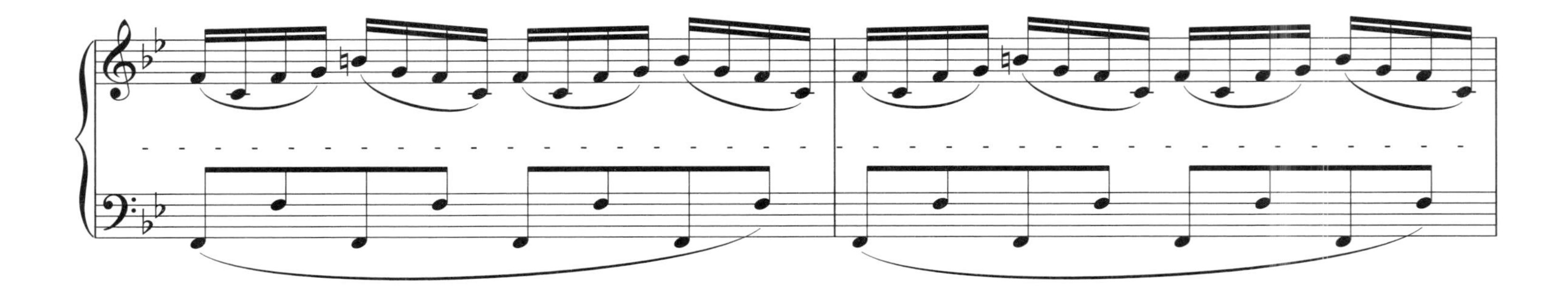
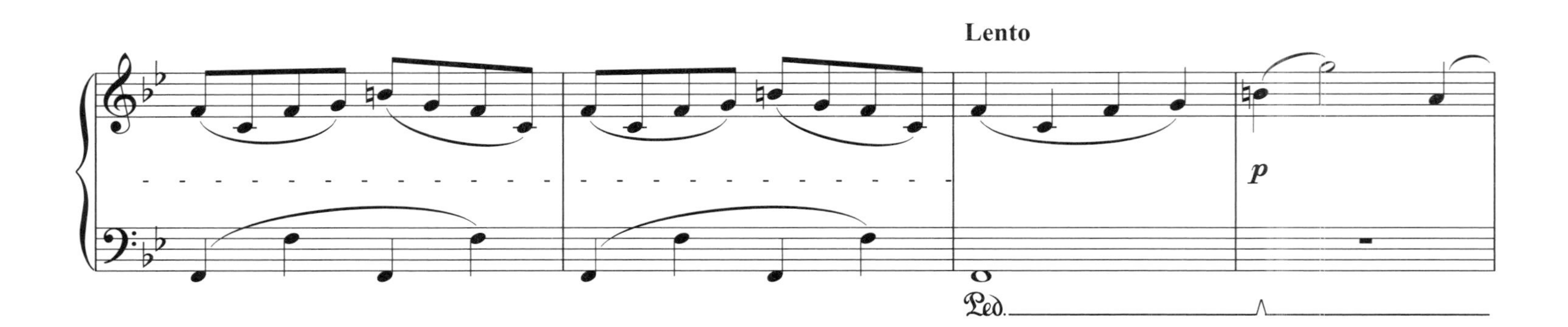
Lento
p
Ped.
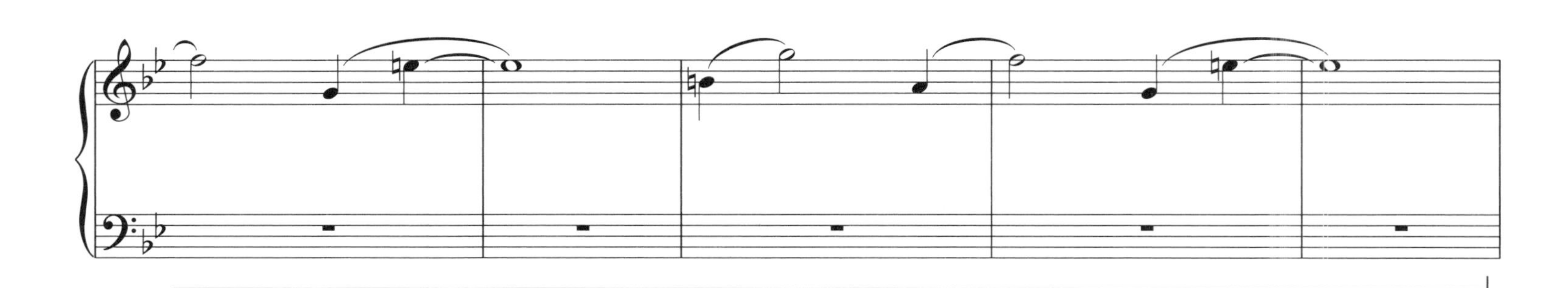

a tempo

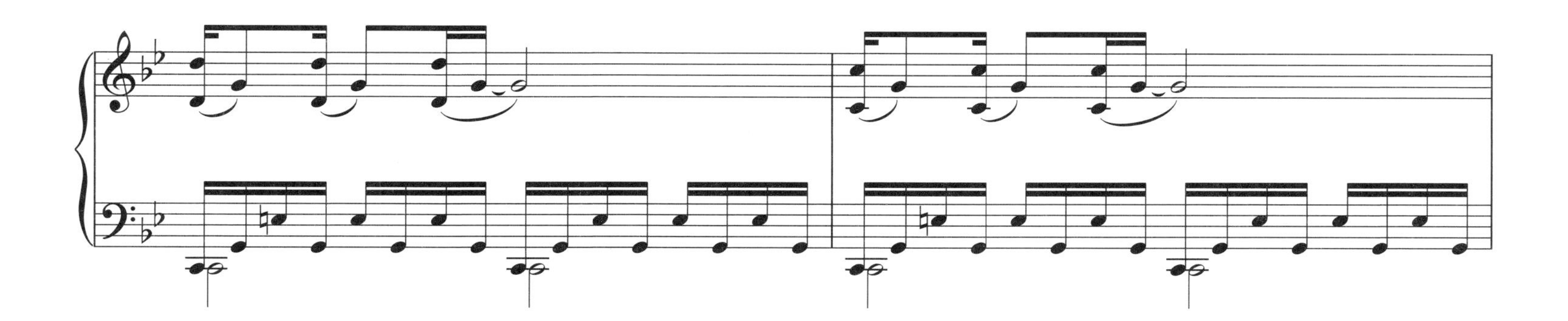

rall.

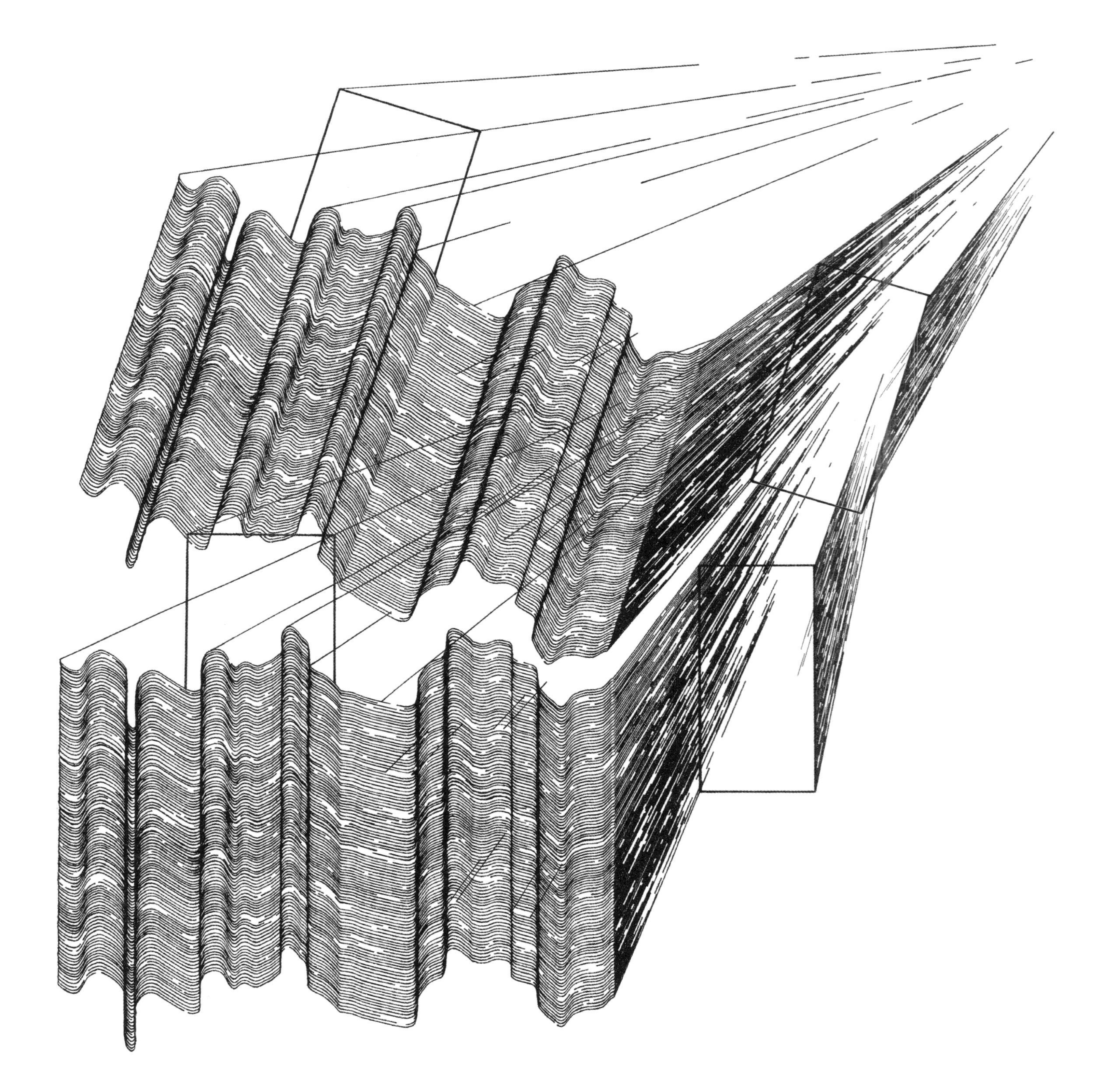

Kerber

MUSIC BY YANN TIERSEN

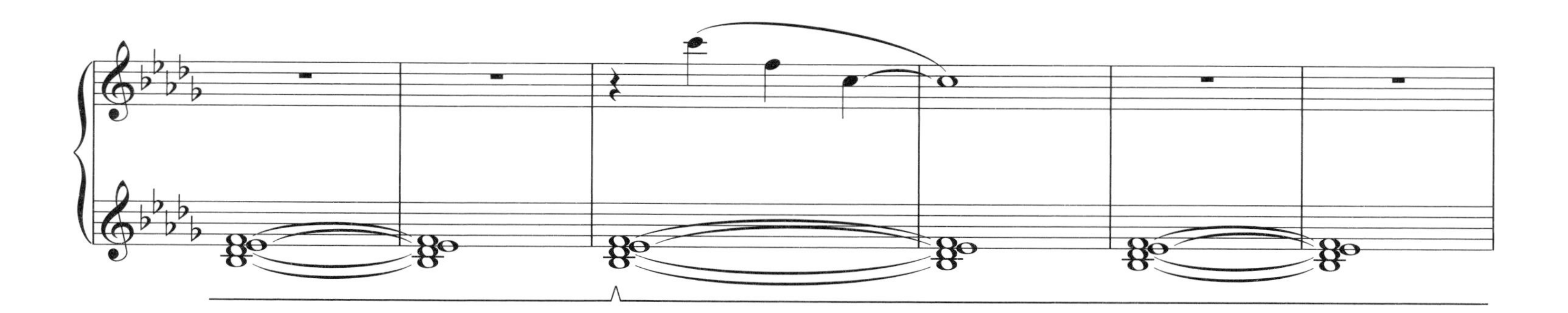

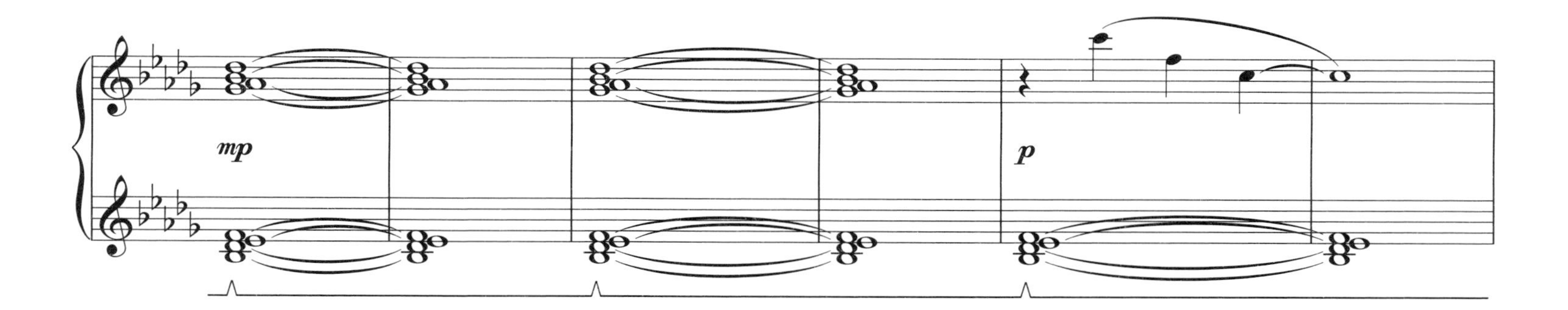

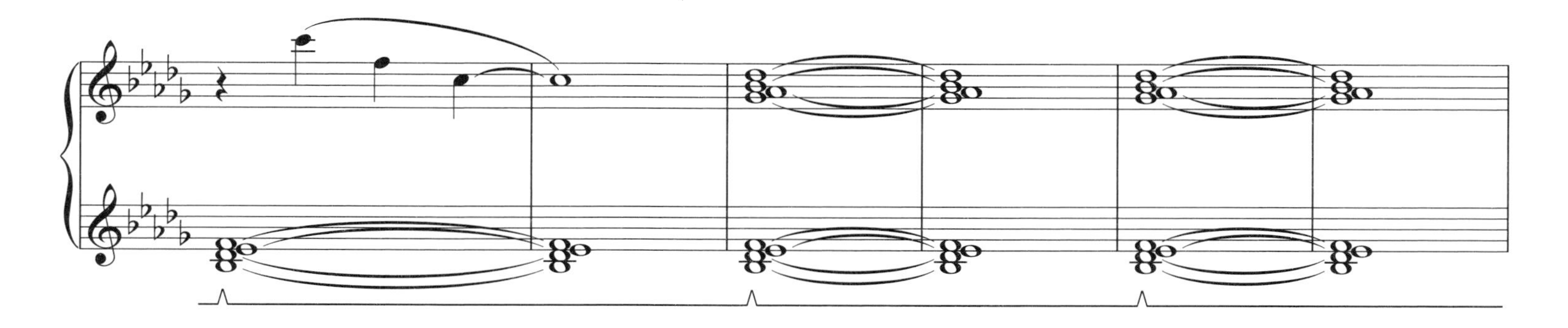

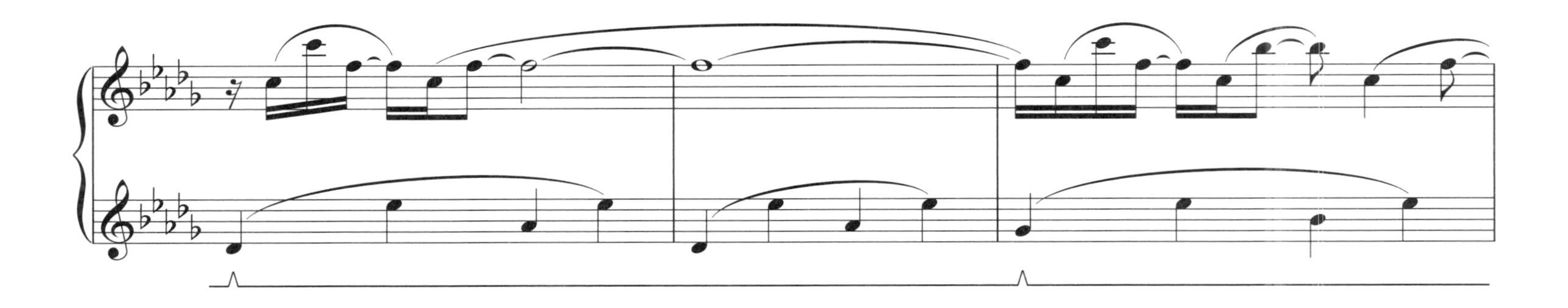

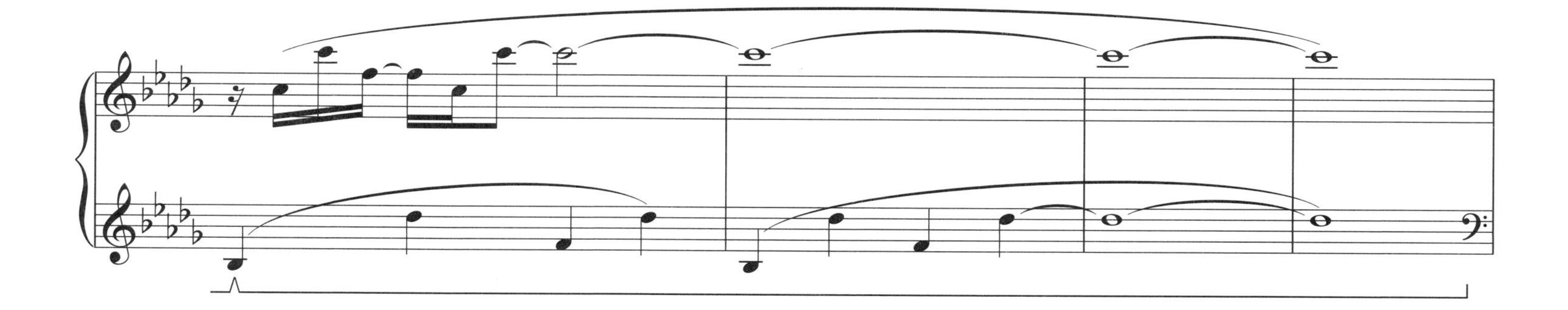

mf
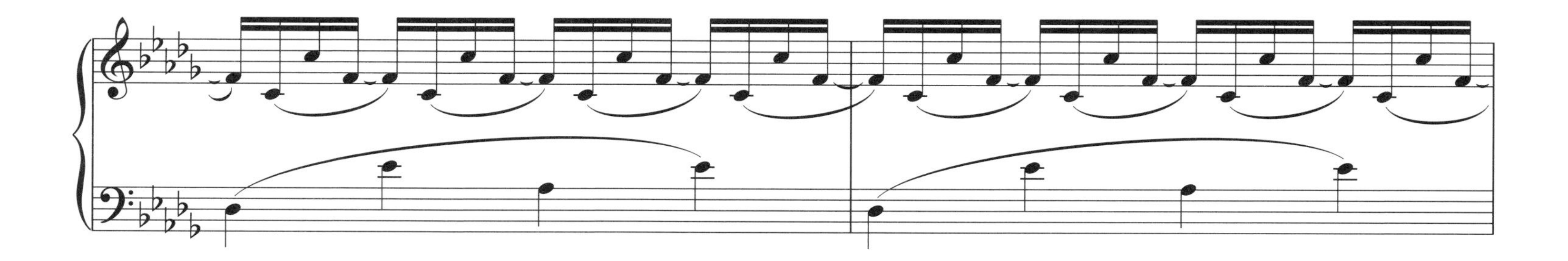
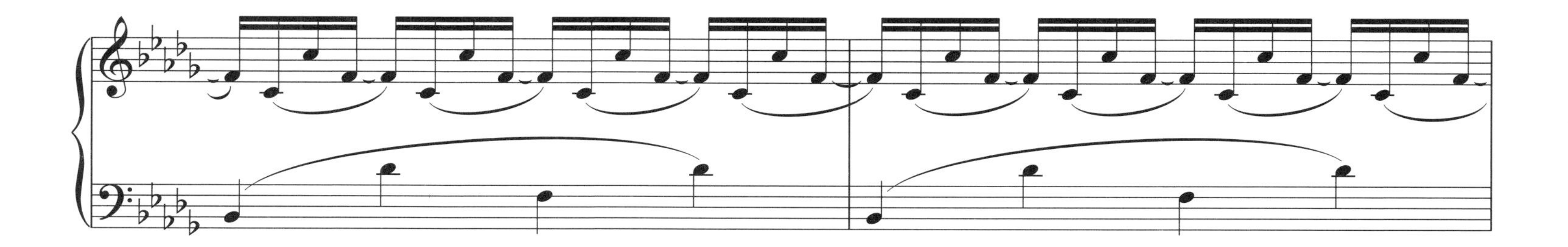

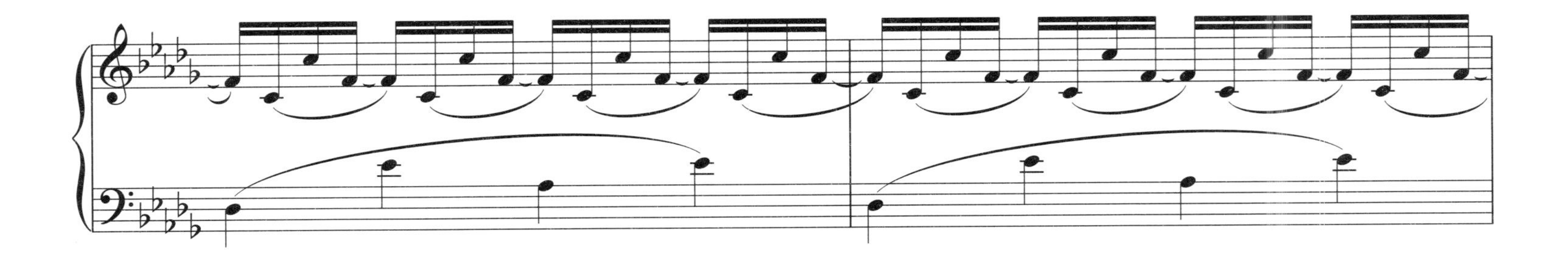

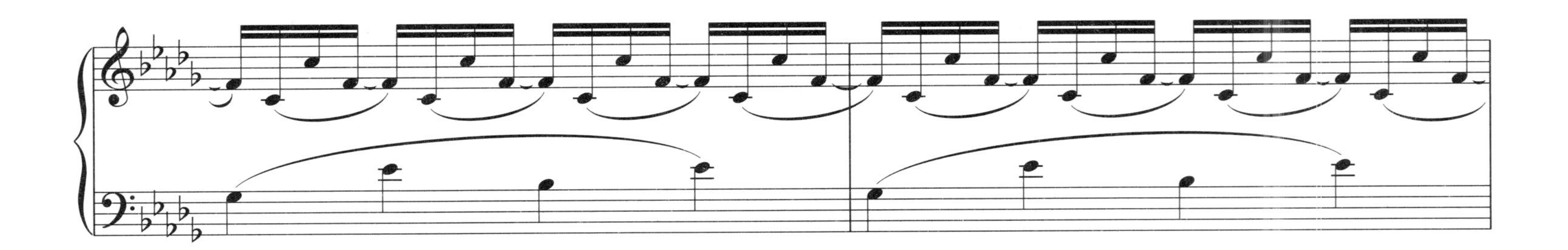

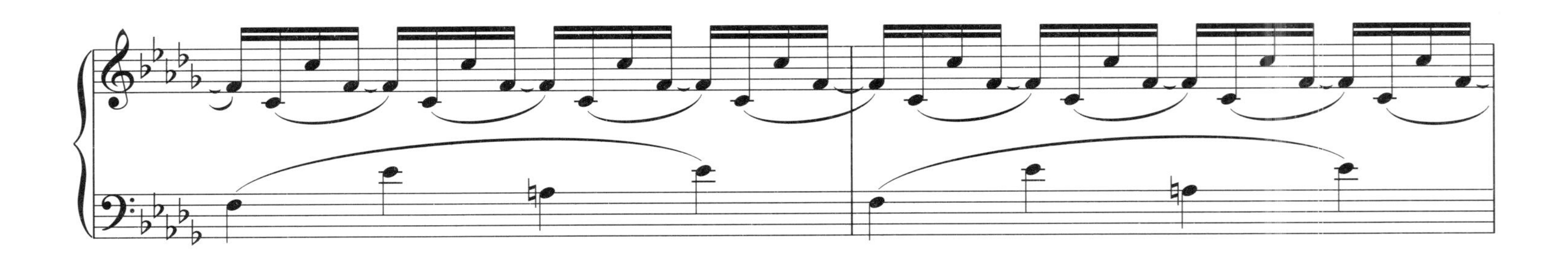

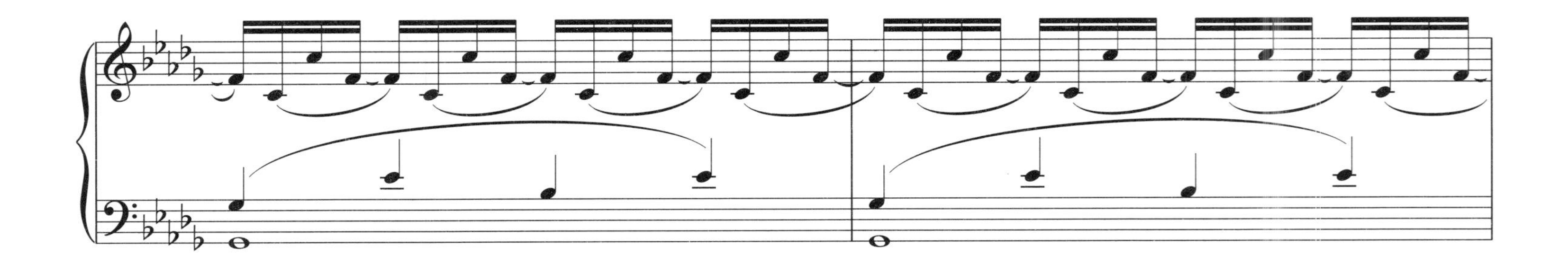

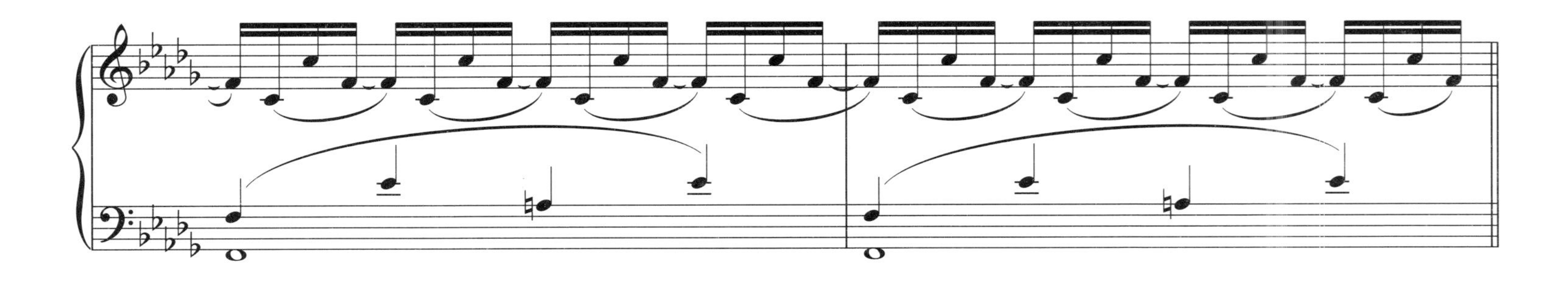

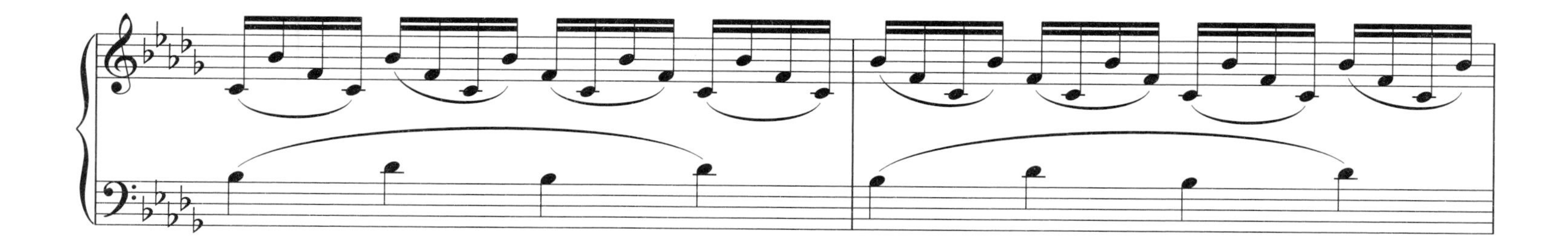

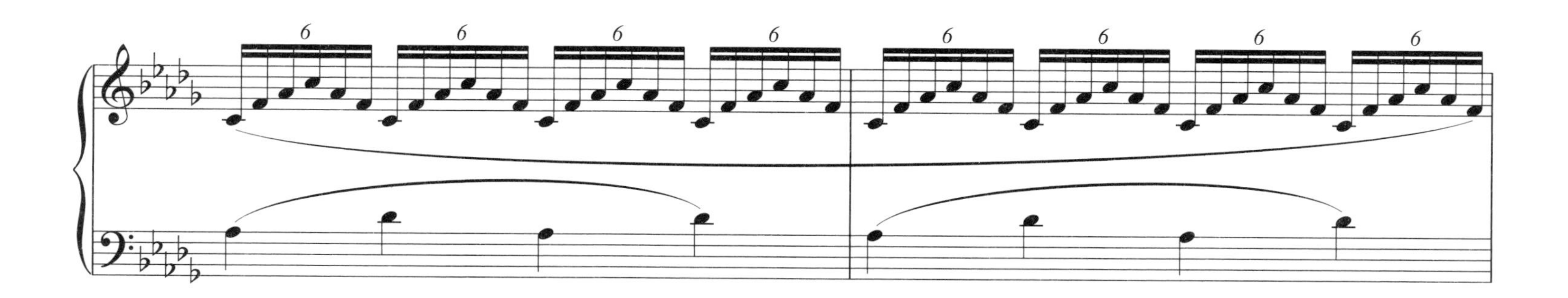

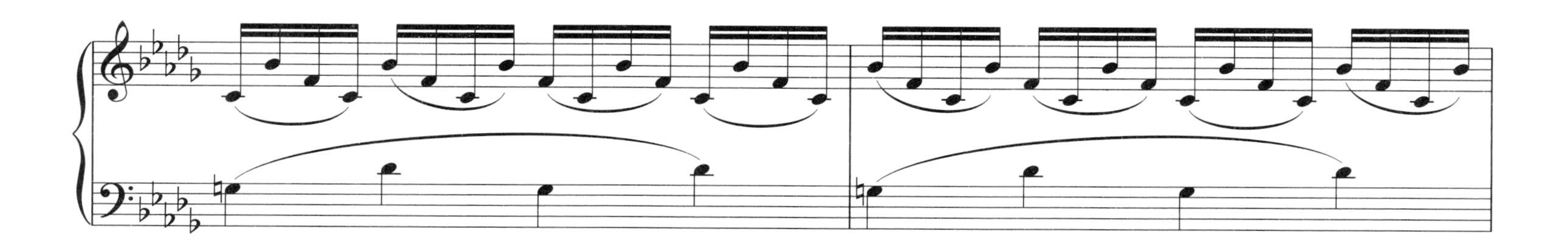

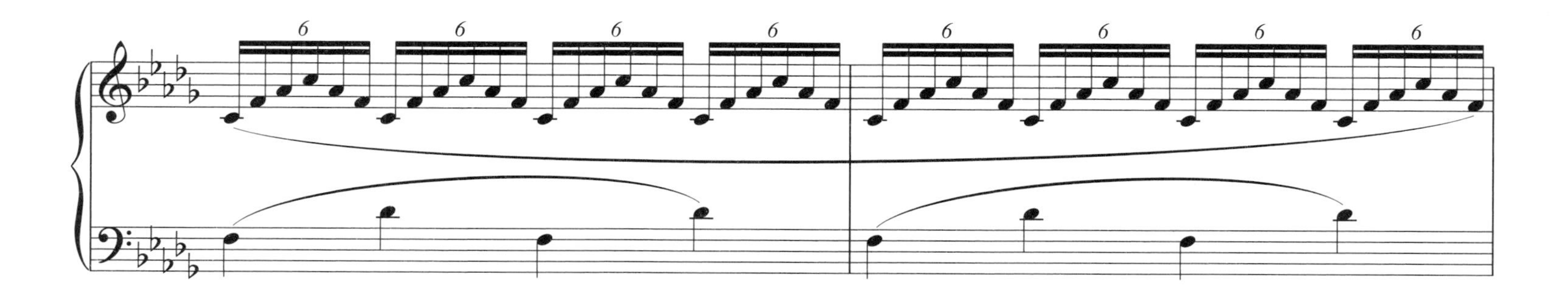

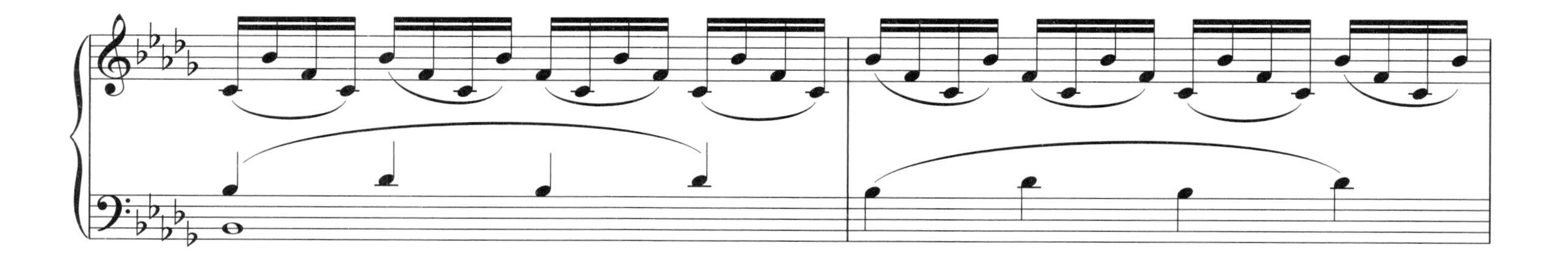

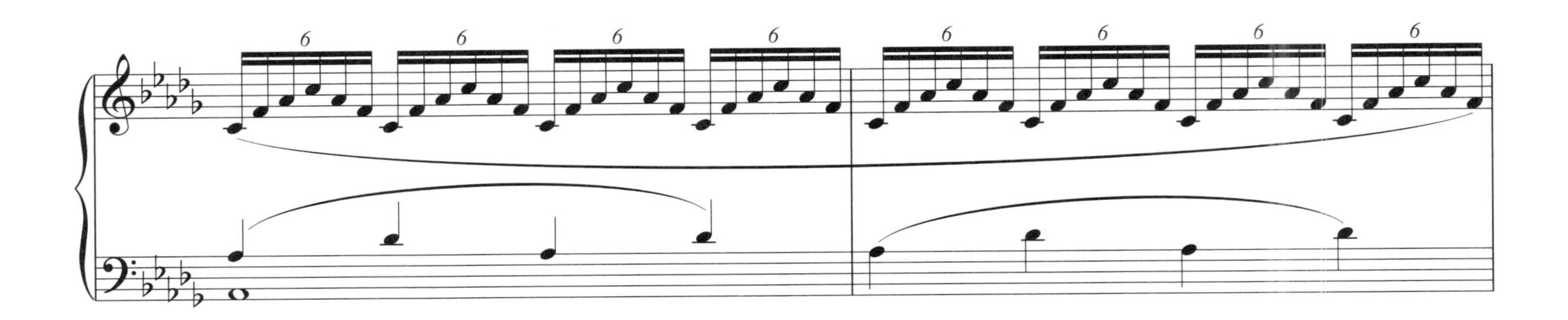

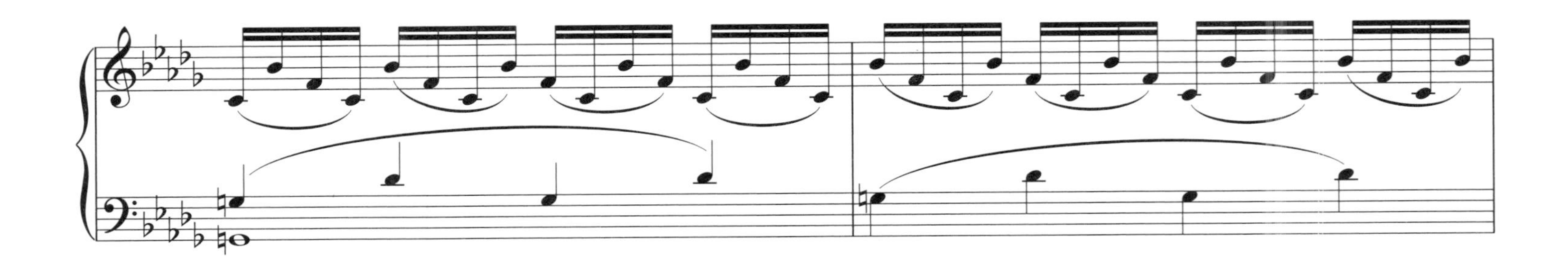

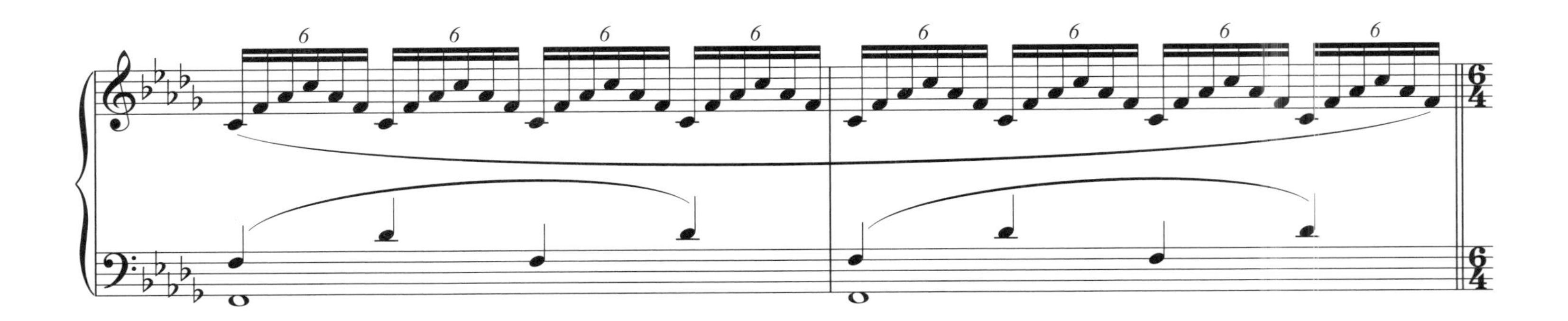

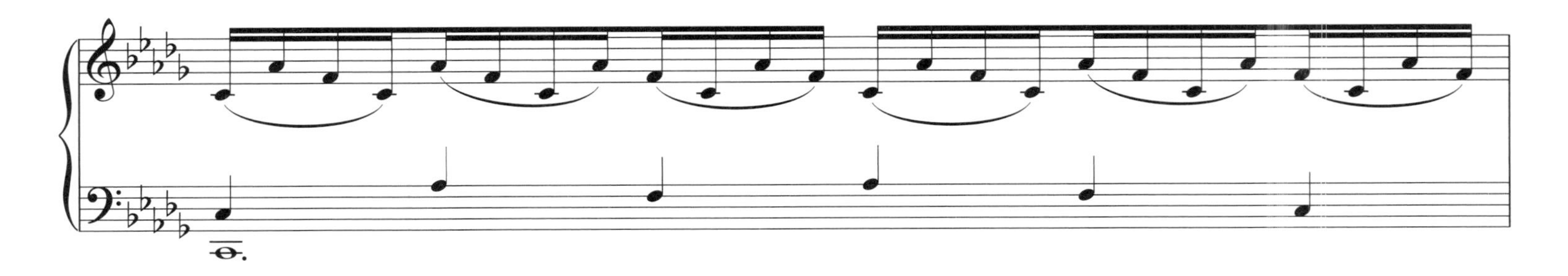

6
6
6
6
6
6

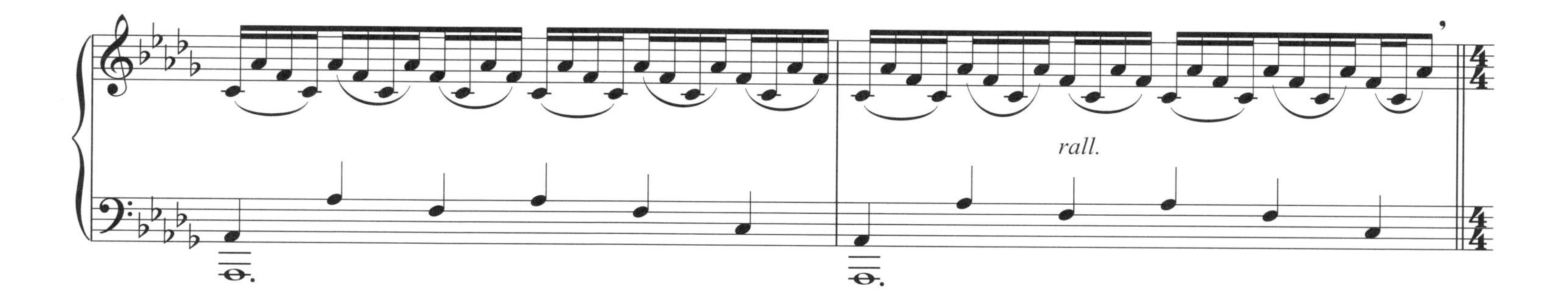

rall.

p a tempo
Ped.
Ped. cont. sim.

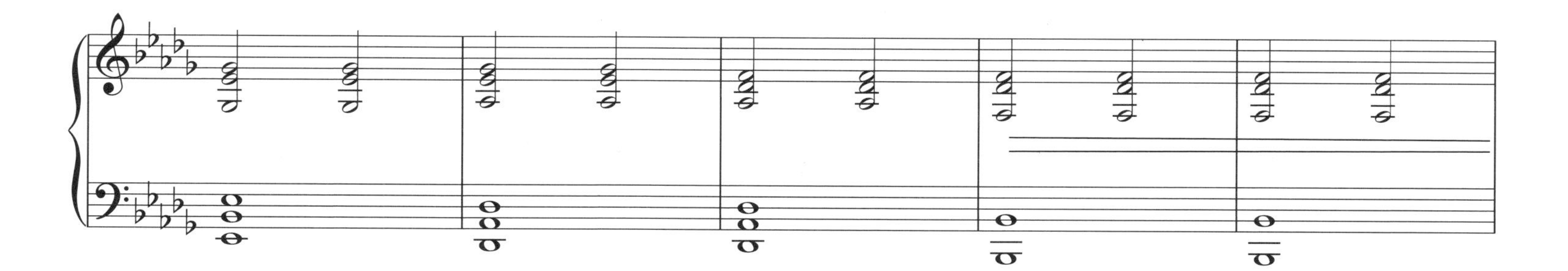

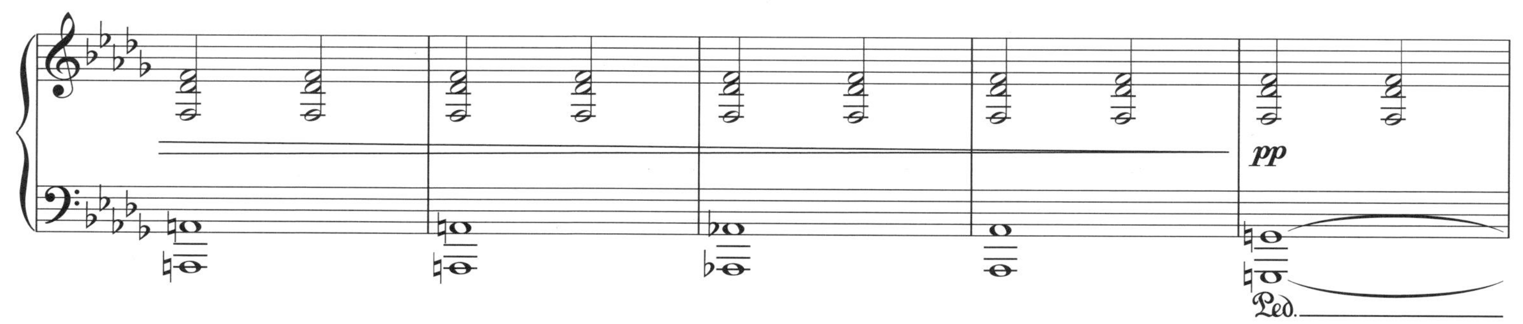

pp
Ped.

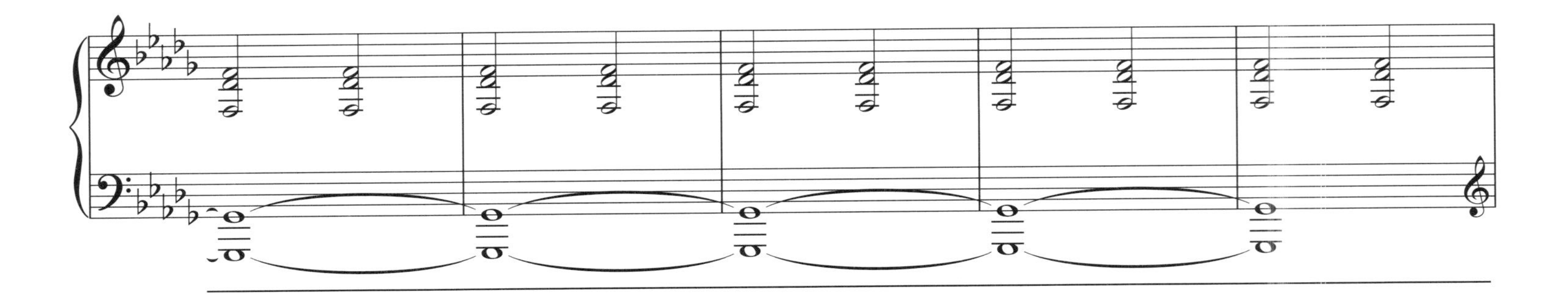
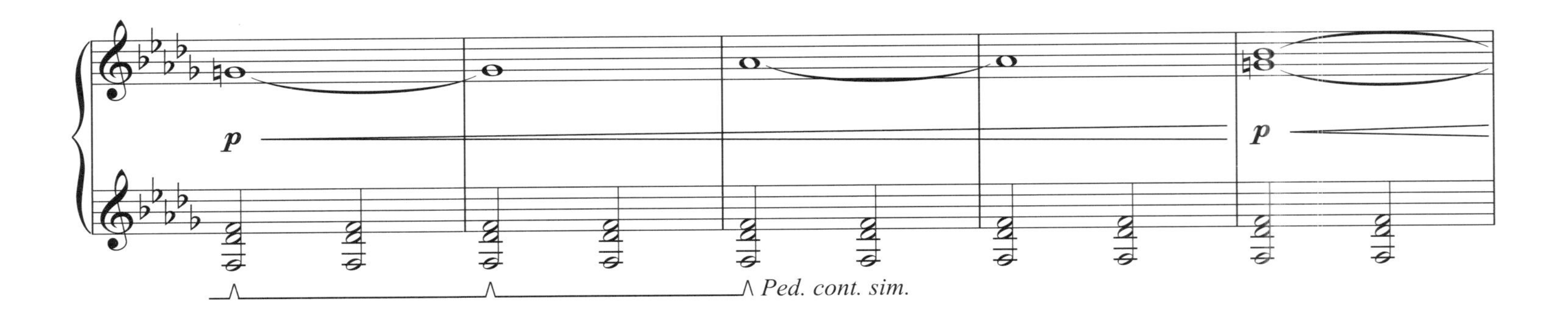
p
p
Ped. cont. sim.
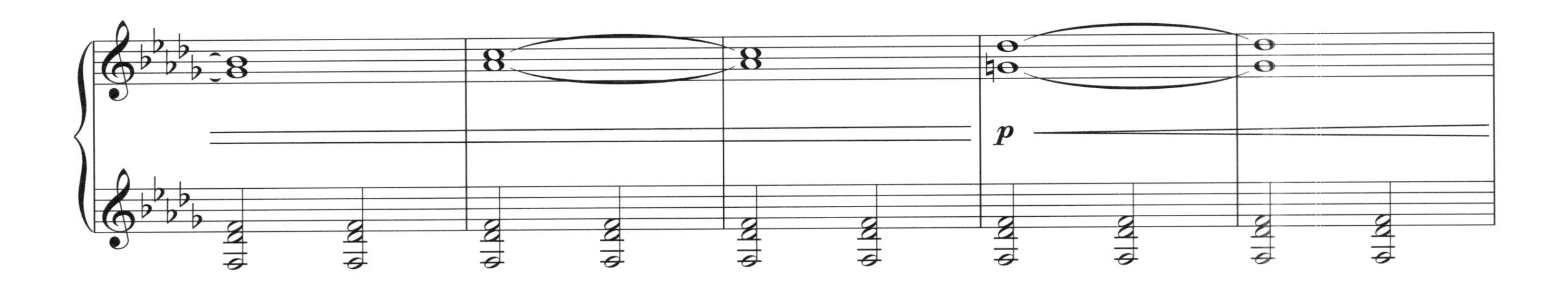
p
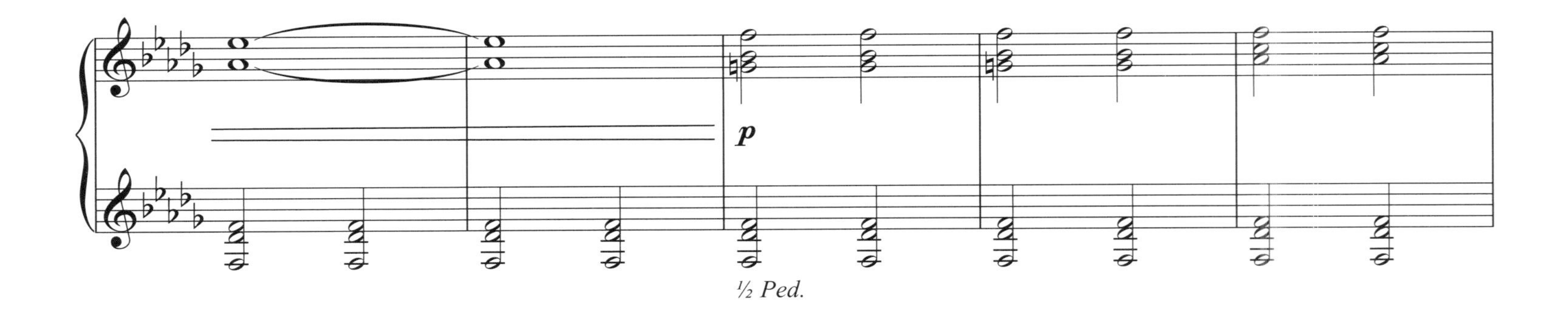
p
½ Ped.

𝅗𝅥 = 60
Ped.
Ped. cont. sim.

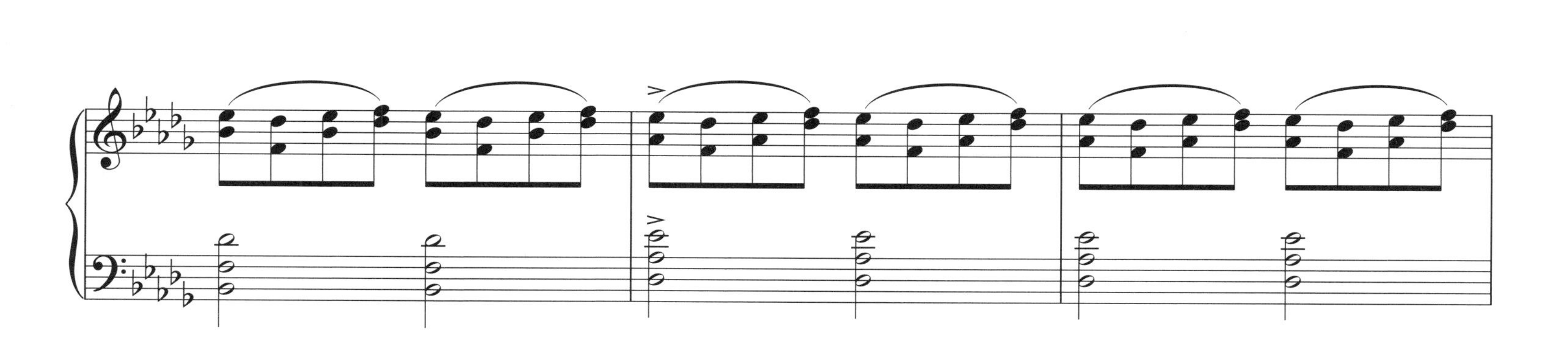

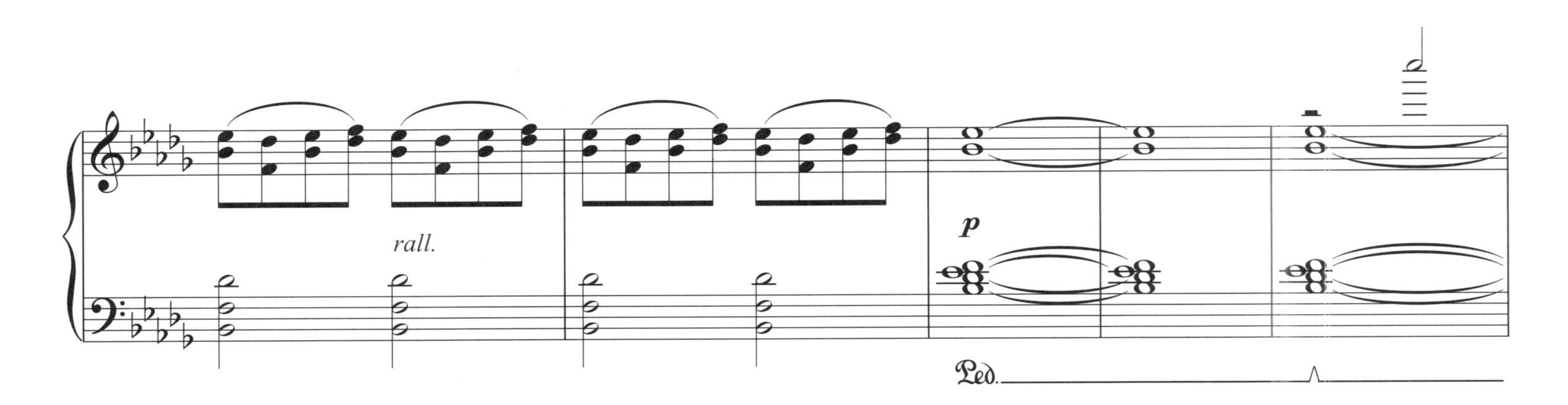
rall.
p
Ped.

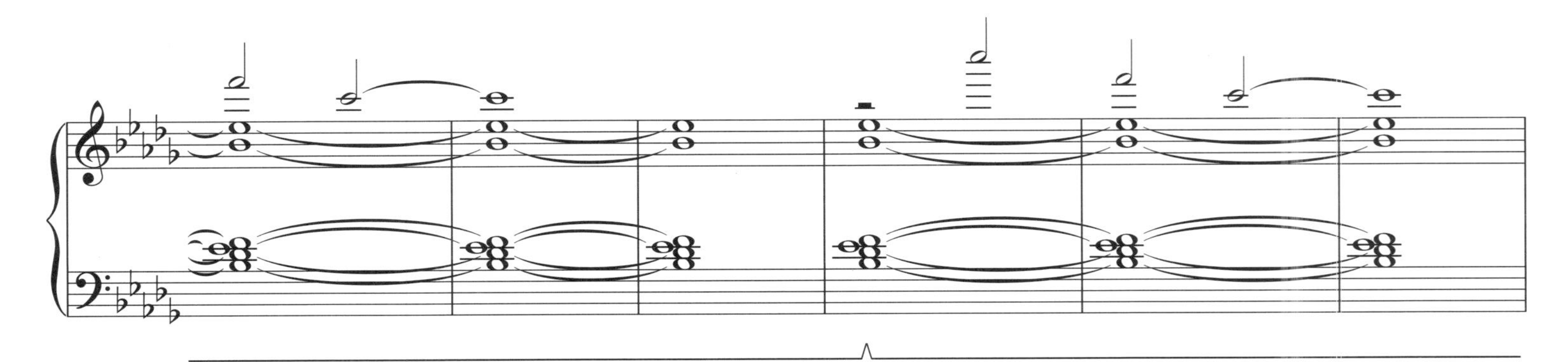

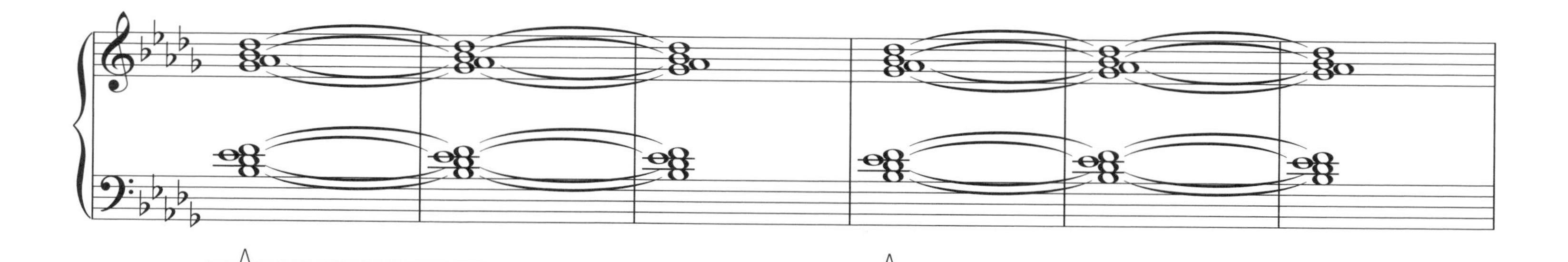
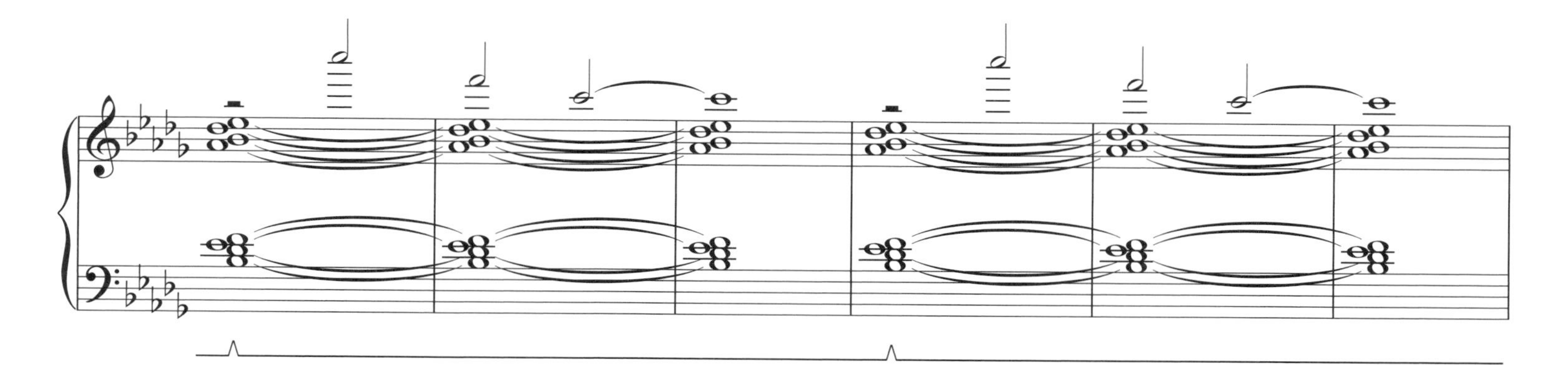
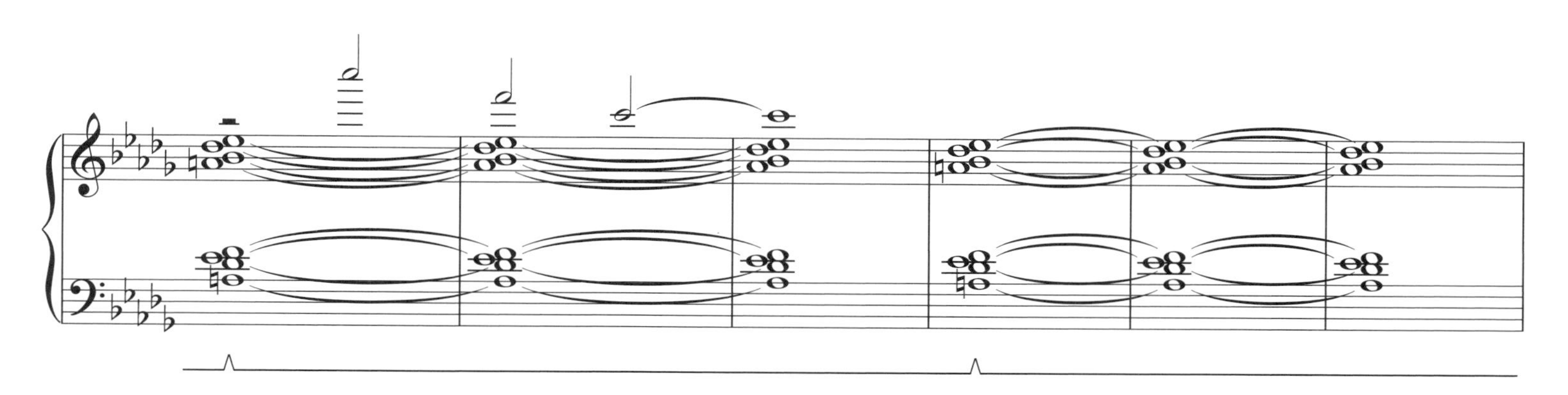

p a tempo

Ped. cont. sim.

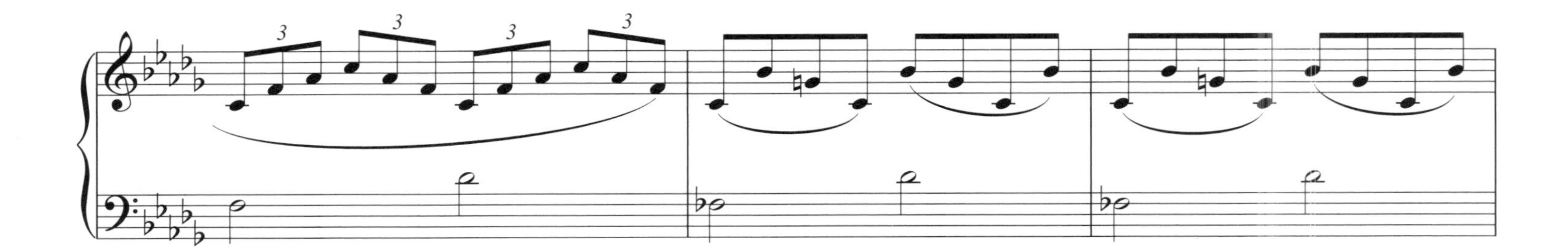

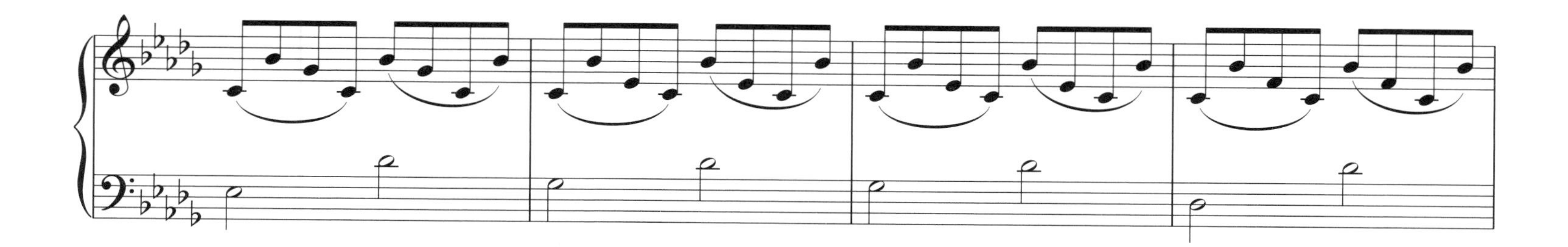
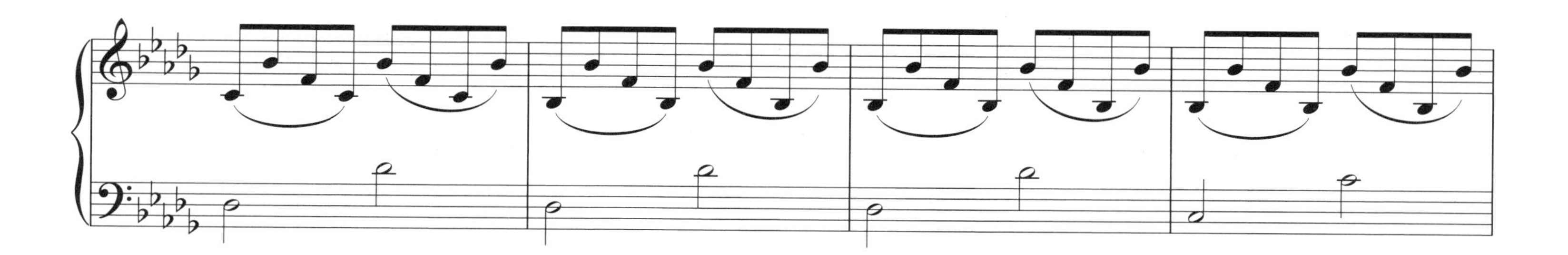
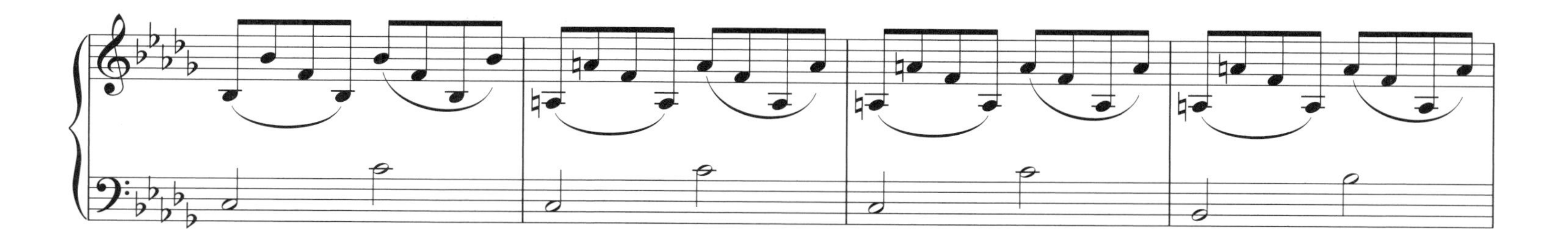

Poull Bojer

MUSIC BY YANN TIERSEN

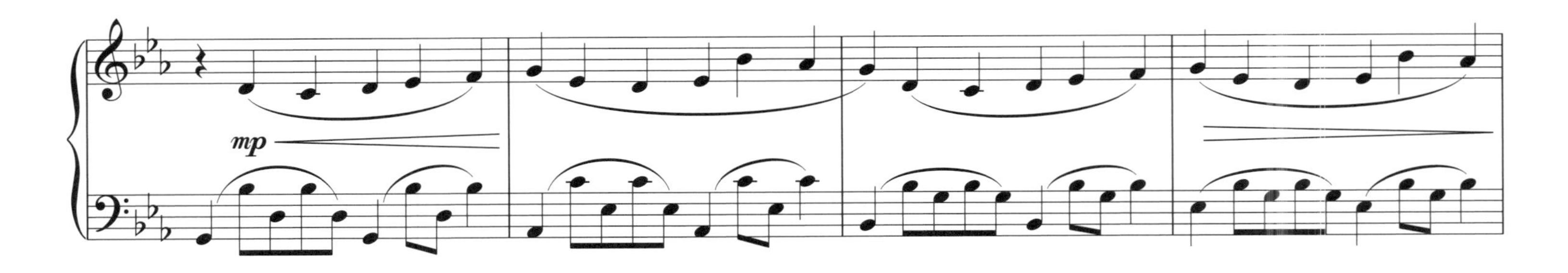

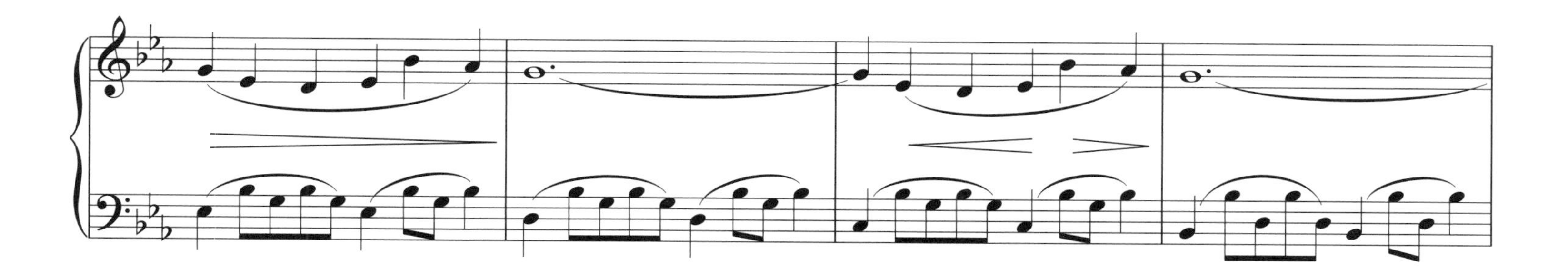

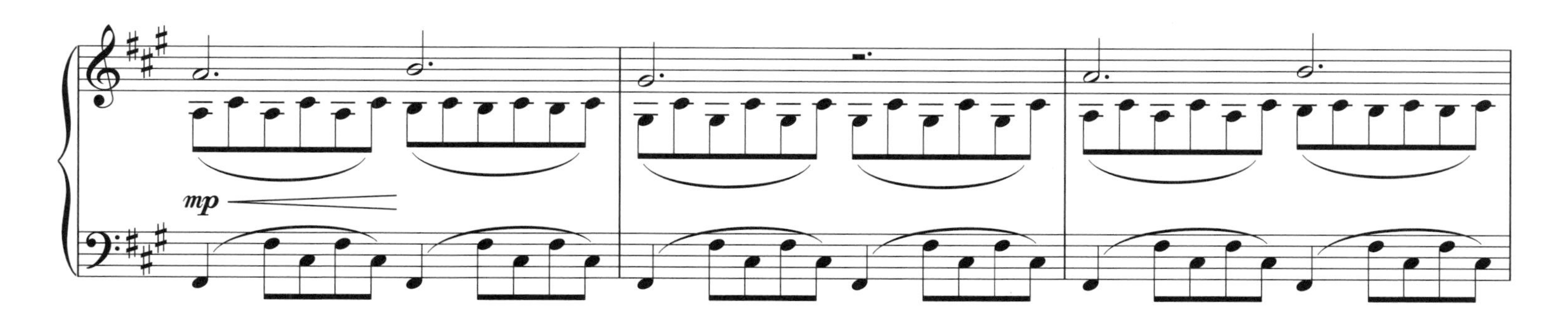
mp

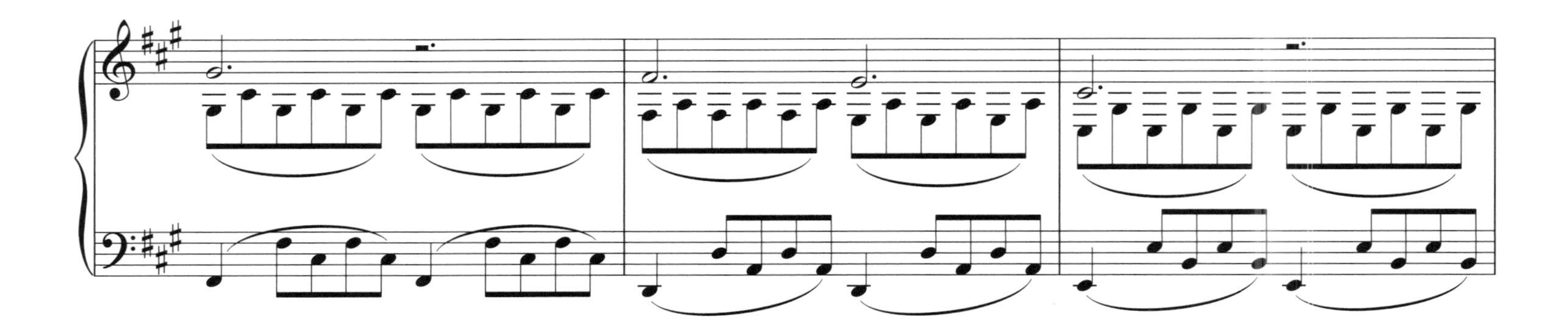

mp

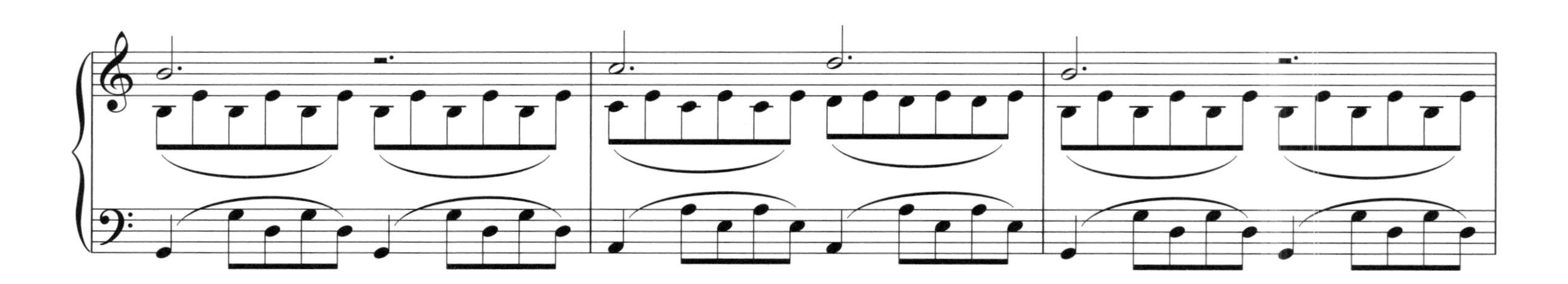

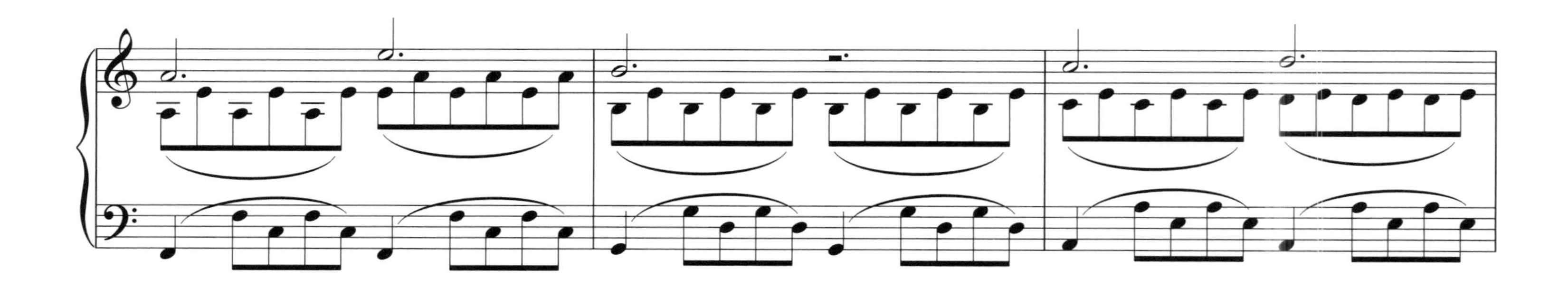

p

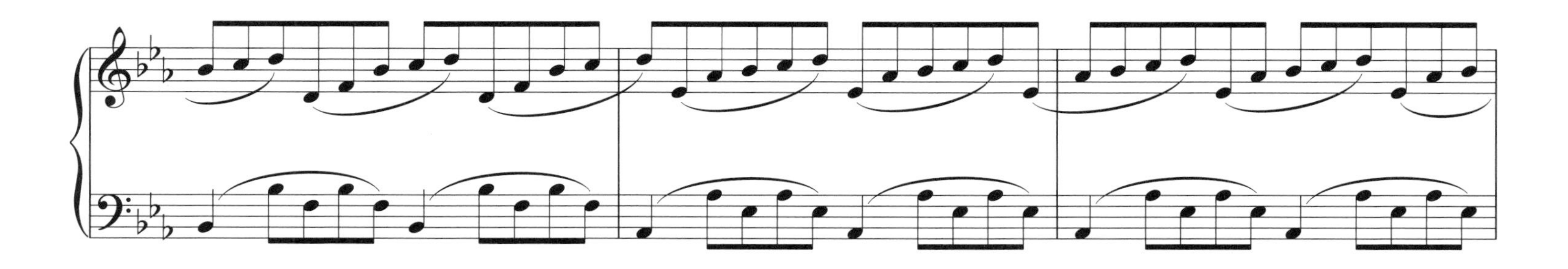

mp

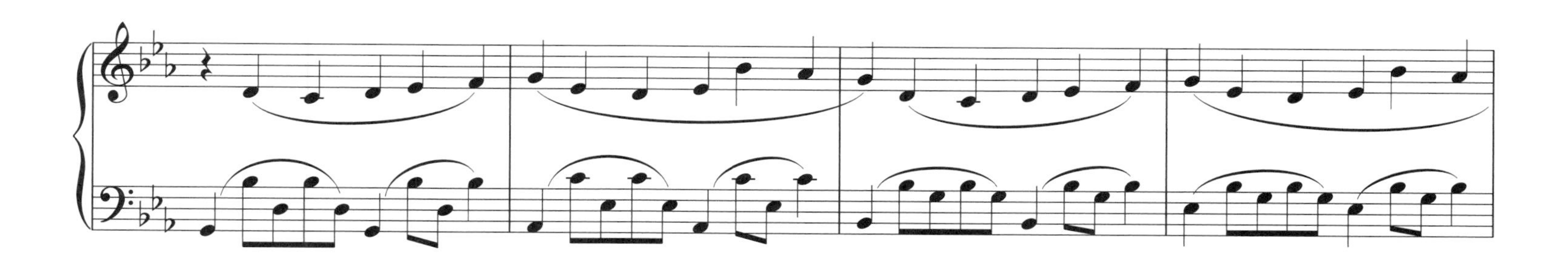

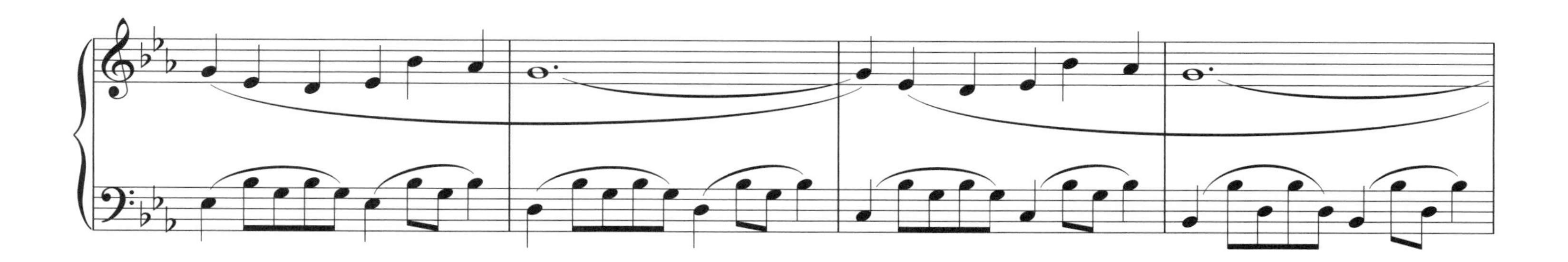

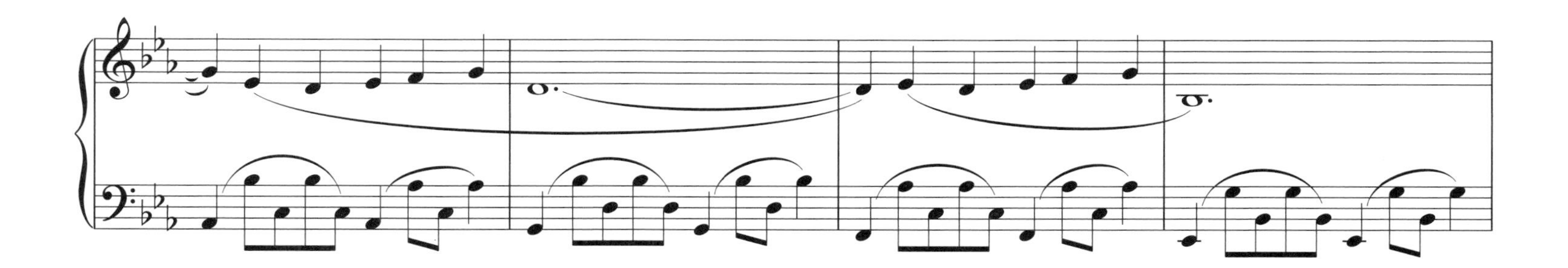

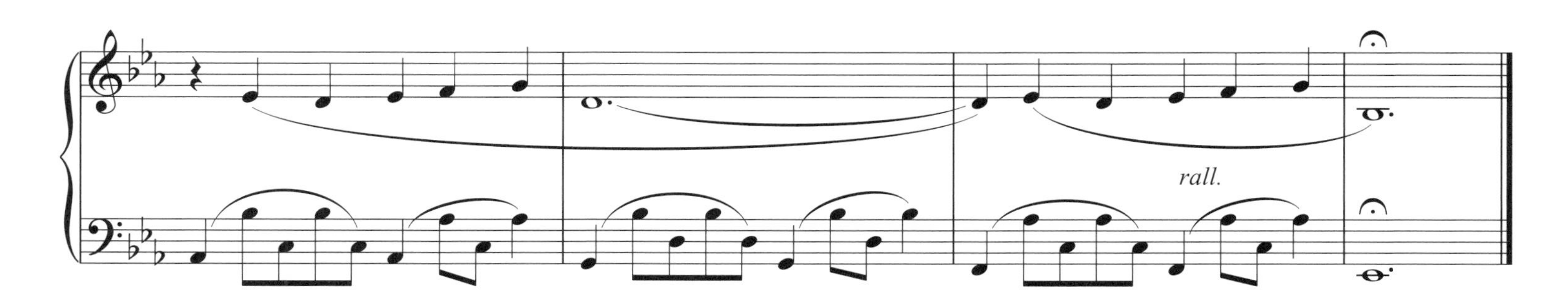
rall.